Migration and socioeconomic change

Available in other formats

This publication can be provided in other formats, such as large print, Braille and audio. Please contact: Communications, Joseph Rowntree Foundation, The Homestead, 40 Water End, York YO30 6WP. Tel: 01904 615905. Email: info@jrf.org.uk

Migration and socioeconomic change

A 2001 Census analysis of Britain's larger cities

Tony Champion, Mike Coombes, Simon Raybould and Colin Wymer

JOSEPH ROWNTREE
FOUNDATION

First published in Great Britain in 2007 by

The Policy Press
Fourth Floor, Beacon House
Queen's Road
Bristol BS8 1QU
UK

Tel no +44 (0)117 331 4054
Fax no +44 (0)117 331 4093
Email tpp-info@bristol.ac.uk
www.policypress.org.uk

Published for the Joseph Rowntree Foundation by The Policy Press

ISBN 978 1 84742 003 9

British Library Cataloguing in Publication Data
A catalogue record for this book is available from the British Library.

Library of Congress Cataloging-in-Publication Data
A catalog record for this book has been requested.

Tony Champion is Emeritus Professor of Population Geography, **Mike Coombes** is Professor of Geographic Information, **Simon Raybould** is Senior Research Associate and **Colin Wymer** is a freelance researcher. All the authors are associated with CURDS (Centre for Urban and Regional Development Studies) in the University of Newcastle upon Tyne where this research was carried out.

The **Joseph Rowntree Foundation** has supported this project as part of its programme of research and innovative development projects, which it hopes will be of value to policy makers, practitioners and service users. The facts presented and views expressed in this report are, however, those of the authors and not necessarily those of the Foundation.

Cover photograph supplied by Doug Hall, i2i Photography (www.i-two-i.co.uk)
Cover design by Qube Design Associates, Bristol
Printed in Great Britain by Latimer Trend, Plymouth

Contents

List of tables, figures and maps

Tables

Figures

Maps

Acknowledgements

The Joseph Rowntree Foundation funded the research reported here as part of its programme of projects concerned with the analysis of data from the 2001 Census. Data from the Census of population is Crown Copyright, reproduced with the permission of the Controller of HMSO.

The authors are very grateful for the support and advice given by the Foundation's Anne Harrop and, latterly, Kathleen Kelly. Thanks are also due to the project's advisory group who provided the authors with ideas, comments and encouragement throughout the study. Its members were Nick Bailey, Barbara Ballard, Glen Bramley, Tim Butler, Sarah Fielder, Tony Fielding, John Hollis, Cecilia McIntyre, John Stillwell and Frank Thomas.

Glossary

MGRP	Moving group reference person: moving group refers to either one person moving on their own or two or more people who had been living at the same previous address before moving together to their usual address at the time of the census. If there is only one person in the moving group, that person is the MGRP. If the moving group contains the household reference person (HRP), the MGRP is the HRP. If the HRP is not in the moving group, the MGRP is chosen from among any family reference person (FRP) using the criteria of economic activity, then age, then order on the form. If there is no FRP, the MGRP is chosen from among any people in generation 1 of a family using the same criteria.
NHS	National Health Service: data from the NHS Central Register, derived from patients' registrations with their doctors, provides a continuous record of people changing address and forms the principal basis of data on within-UK migration used for the annual population estimates.
NS-SEC	National Statistics Socioeconomic Classification: this is the 2001 Census equivalent of SEG (Socioeconomic Group) as used in previous censuses. See Appendix A for more details.
ONS	Office for National Statistics: the agency responsible for undertaking the UK population census in England and Wales, alongside the General Register Office (Scotland) and the Northern Ireland Statistical and Research Agency.
PUA	Primary urban area: the starting point for the definition of PUAs was the set of physical urban area boundaries defined by the ONS and used for reporting 2001 Census data. Cities in different labour market areas (as identified by travel-to-work areas) and that had only tangentially linked built-up areas – like Leeds and Bradford – were kept separate.
SMS	Special migration statistics: the SMS form part of the origin destination statistics of the 2001 Census. For three sets of geographies (district, ward and output area levels), they provide counts of migration flows between each area of the UK and every other area, broken down by selected characteristics of the migrants. These breakdowns are fewer and/or have less detailed categories in the datasets reporting for the finer geographies.

Summary

This report presents the results of an analysis of within-UK migration in the year leading up to the 2001 Census and aims to discover whether 27 large British cities were attracting more migrants from elsewhere in the country than they were losing. The analyses separate out migration over longer distances from that between cities and the remainder of their own city regions. In three city regions – London, Birmingham and Bristol – more local patterns of movement are examined to see whether or not this migration is increasing socioeconomic polarisation.

The *key message* from the report is as follows:

- Compared to studies based on the two previous censuses, this analysis of the 2001 Census migration data paints a somewhat more favourable picture for urban Britain in aggregate, but this is primarily due to London's great attraction for the most skilled migrants.

Other important *findings* are as follows:

- More cities lost population as a result of within-UK migration than gained, but their combined net loss of 63,000 people was mainly accounted for by London's large loss.
- Only 9 of the 27 cities made a net gain of 'moving groups' through their longer-distance migration exchanges, and only 10 received more from the rest of their city regions than they lost.
- London saw very many more 'Higher managerial and professional' people arriving than leaving, but most cities appear less successful at attracting and/or keeping this key group than they are with migrants in general.
- Most cities making the strongest gains from long-distance migration had seen local job growth and also possess a range of features associated with a higher quality of life.
- The least attractive cities for longer-distance flows also tend to suffer the highest losses to other parts of their regions; this pattern can lead to housing market weakness.
- Within the three case study city regions, selective migration has a marginal tendency to reinforce existing social differences between localities: thus within the London and Bristol regions, 'Higher managerial and professional' people tend to move to areas with higher average incomes, and in Birmingham and Bristol to areas where semi-detached house prices rose more quickly.
- Students moving to university boosted most of the 27 cities' populations, but the departure of recent graduates weakens most provincial cities' growth potential, although the census does not permit a precise assessment of this.

The *significance* of these findings can be summarised as follows:

- Within-UK migration is still acting as a mechanism for supplying labour where and when it is needed (note that the census data analysed here pre-dates the recent surge of migration from East and Central Europe that may have supplanted some within-UK labour migration flows).
- While this economic driver is particularly clear for cities' longer-distance migration, it now also seems to apply to cities' migration exchanges with the rest of their own city regions, with people moving to the economically stronger localities.
- It remains the case that it is the higher skill occupations that are the more responsive to these labour market drivers, reflecting the increasing premium that they command in the growing knowledge-based industries.
- London's domination of these migration flows appears at least as great as in the past, posing a continuing threat to the sustainability of the recent positive shifts in migration balance towards many northern cities.
- This suggests that policies designed to reinforce the economic transformation of cities and improve their attractiveness as places to live need to be pursued even more imaginatively and energetically in the future.

At the same time, there remains a need for more detailed and robust intelligence on these population movements. The report puts forward three main areas for attention:

- There is a strong case for the *continuous monitoring of migration* by labour market position and skill level, rather than relying on the 10-yearly snapshot from the census, so as to provide a more frequent check on city performance.
- The migration data, as well as much else from the census, would be greatly enhanced by the *collection of information on people's labour market position* one year ago.
- The *lack of occupational mobility data* in the census – and the problems caused by not identifying recent graduates – leads to the need for research using the ONS Longitudinal Study to examine people's residential movement and socioeconomic progression.

1

Introduction

Urban Britain seems to be enjoying something of a recovery. In recent years there have been upward shifts in population growth rate, widespread falls in unemployment levels and signs of renewed interest in cities as a place to live. For those concerned with urban regeneration, this is a very welcome change from previous experience, especially that of the 1970s when in just 10 years London lost three quarters of a million people and the six next largest cities lost a total in excess of half a million (Champion and Fisher, 2004). Yet there is clear statistical evidence that the principal urban areas are continuing to lose people to the smaller cities, towns and rural areas that make up the rest of the country. Indeed, as shown in this report (Chapter 2), the net exodus from metropolitan England has been running at a particularly high level since the turn of the century.

It might be argued that, if cities appear to have turned the corner in terms of overall population growth, due to factors such as a high birth rate or inflows of migrants from abroad, a continuing urban exodus should not cause concern. After all, people are presumably 'voting with their feet' in the quest for a better life, and they are leaving cities because they are less successful at providing what they want at an acceptable level of cost. Moreover, planning restrictions – not just 'greenbelts' limiting the lateral extension of the built-up area but also conservation measures designed to protect the best features of the urban environment – can mean that housebuilding is unable to keep up with a city's growth in household numbers.

Set against this argument, however, are several considerations affecting the future prospects for cities as places where large numbers of people live. In the first place, the two current sources of urban population growth – natural increase (the surplus of births over deaths) and net immigration from overseas – may not continue in the longer term. In any case, if there were to be even just a slowing of the net exodus from the cities then this would help to accelerate the process of urban recovery. As is made clear in the report *The state of the English cities* (Parkinson et al, 2006), the urban recovery has so far been a decidedly patchy affair, with many cities still registering overall population decline. These cities need to achieve a more positive balance in their migration exchanges with the rest of the UK just to reach the point where they can maintain their population numbers.

Going beyond these arguments about bald numbers, the urban exodus also prompts concern on other very important grounds. Migration tends to be a selective process that involves some types of people much more than others. Traditionally, the net out-migration from cities – just like the long-established patterns of suburbanisation from older urban cores to the growing suburbs (Champion, 2002) – has been predominantly a movement of wealthier people. Previous research on the migration losses of Britain's main conurbations based on the 1981 and 1991 Censuses revealed a quite consistent association between rates of loss and levels of social status, such that these cities were losing disproportionately large numbers of professionals and managers and far fewer low-skill manual workers (Champion and Fisher, 2003).

This socially selective form of migration raises at least two major concerns for policy makers, as spelt out for England's cities in the Rogers Report (1999) and the government's subsequent proposals for achieving an 'urban renaissance' (DETR, 2000). This remains a major concern in Britain, with particular attention now being focused on how to tackle the emergence of low-demand housing areas and how to combat social exclusion more generally (SEU, 1998; Bramley et al, 2000).

The other, more recently recognised, issue concerns the threat that this migration is now widely seen as posing to the long-term sustainability of cities' economic bases. As the knowledge economy has become more important in national growth, urban regeneration can also be seen as depending on the development of the 'creative industries' and, along with this, on the attraction and retention of the highly qualified workers on which this sector relies (Florida, 2002). To the extent that the urban exodus involves the movement of such people beyond the commuting range of cities' employment centres, it makes far more difficult the task of securing a long-term transformation of their economies.

It is this more policy-critical dimension of the selectivity of the migration exchanges between cities and the rest of Britain that forms the primary focus of this study. The overriding aim of our research has been to obtain new insights into the extent and ways in which migration is affecting the nation's larger cities. In particular, we have examined whether the demographic and economic recovery of urban Britain since the early 1990s has been accompanied by any alteration in the traditional relationship between occupational skill level and net out-migration, even if there does not seem to have been any diminution in the overall volume of this movement.

Among the questions addressed in this report, therefore, are the following:

- Is out-migration from the larger cities to the rest of the UK still skewed towards the more skilled and higher social status groups?
- How far is this exodus due to people moving out to nearby areas, as opposed to longer-distance migration to other parts of the country?
- What differences are there in the social complexion of the cities' more local population exchanges compared with their longer distance ones?
- Which types of localities have the most in-migration of the more highly skilled, and how far is migration reinforcing the existing distribution of this group?

Accompanying all these questions is the degree to which individual cities differ in these respects, as opposed to all of urban Britain following the same trajectory. To the extent that there is variation, what does this appear to be linked to?

Our study has been based almost entirely on the 2001 Census of population. No other source can match the decennial census as a source of data on people moving to, from, and within cities. It features a unique combination of virtually 100% coverage of the population and wealth of information about each person, with some of the data available for a fine grain of areas. In particular, it provides information on migrants' economic position (for example, employed, unemployed, student) and occupation (from which people's social status and skill group can be gauged). By contrast, other migration data sources either do not collect this sort of information about the characteristics of migrants or have a sample size that is too small to allow estimates to be made confidently at the city level (Bulusu, 1991; Rees et al, 2002).

In looking at the data from the latest census, the report provides not just an updating but also an extension of work carried out on the 1981 and 1991 Censuses migration data. Most notably, taking advantage of the much greater geographical detail that the 2001 Census provides on the social complexion of between-place migration, the present study examines a considerably larger number of cities than was previously possible. In not being constrained to using large county-level areas, we define our cities on the basis of their main built-up areas, or at least the best-fit of local authority areas to these (see Chapter 3). Additionally, with the 2001 Census being the first one to use term-time address as the usual residence of students, the movements of people to, from, and at university are included in the migration data for the first time.

Unfortunately, however, there is also a downside to the improvements introduced in the 2001 Census, namely that the results derived from this study cannot be compared directly with those from previous censuses. As well as the counting of university-related moves for the first time, there are other changes such as the use of a very different socioeconomic classification, the adoption of the 'moving group' concept, more imputation to allow for non-response and a completely different approach to data modification for disclosure control purposes (see Appendix A). As a result, we have not felt able to undertake any formal tests of how the migration patterns observed from the 2001 Census data differ from those found for earlier years. Instead, we merely look for any broad differences in pattern that would appear unlikely to have arisen purely from the definitional and methodological changes.

The difficulty of monitoring trends over time in the social complexion of cities' migration is a topic that we return to in the concluding part of this report (Chapter 6). Next, however, in Chapter 2 we develop the context of this study in more detail, looking at the statistical evidence on urban Britain's population recovery and the role of both international and internal migration in this. The results of our analyses of the 2001 Census migration data are presented in three parts. Chapter 3 examines the migration exchanges between each of the 27 cities and the whole of the rest of the UK, so as to see what form the relationship with social status took in the year leading up to census day (29 April 2001). Chapter 4 then focuses in on the longer-distance component of these exchanges, while the more localised flows – those between the cities and their surrounding 'city regions' – is the subject of Chapter 5. The latter also reports key findings from three case study city regions (London, Birmingham and Bristol), with the main emphasis being on migration flows between each city region's localities and with the primary aim being to see whether these are reinforcing or reducing the inherited social differences there. As such, this complements the work of Bailey and Livingston (2007), which – also part of the Joseph Rowntree Foundation's Census Research Programme – examines the links between migration and deprivation at the much finer grain of census wards and super output areas.

2

Urban population recovery: the statistical evidence

The main purpose of this chapter is to contextualise the findings on migration patterns that are set out in the rest of the report by providing statistical evidence in support of the points made in the introductory chapter. We show the extent to which urban areas have recovered from the severe depopulation of the 1970s, giving particular attention to London and the largest provincial cities. In most cases, this upturn was continuing right up to 2004, the latest year for which data was available at the time of writing, with considerable optimism being expressed about the future prospects for city centre living and a more general 'back to the city' movement. As the rest of the chapter shows, migration is certainly the key to the turnaround in city fortunes, even though natural increase remains the more important component of population growth for large-city Britain as a whole. Generally, however, it is international migration rather than within-UK migration that has been driving the upward shift in population growth rates in recent years. The largest urban areas are continuing to lose population through their migration exchanges with the rest of the country, and the overall volume of this movement has been accelerating since the early 1990s.

Urban population recovery

It is not hard to find statistical evidence of urban recovery. Probably the most comprehensive source is *The state of the English cities* (Parkinson et al, 2006). In aggregate, the 56 cities that were the subject of that report saw their population grow by around half a million people between 1997 and 2003, accounting for 42% of England's overall population growth over this six-year period. While this proportion still fell considerably short of these cities' 58% share of the country's population, it represented a further shift in favour of the cities following the vast improvement in their performance from 1981-91, when their share was barely 7%, to 1991-97, by when it had risen to 36% (Parkinson et al, 2006, vol 2, p 116).

Previously, Champion (2004) had shown how far London and the six former metropolitan counties of England changed in their rates of population growth over the past two decades, shifting from an overall loss of 245,000 people between 1981 and 1991 to an overall gain of 270,000 in the 10 years to 2001. The results of a similar analysis on these counties' core cities, extended to include Glasgow and updated to take account of the latest revisions made to the official estimates for 2001, are presented in Table 2.1. While six of the eight cities still recorded depopulation between 1991 and 2001, there was a fairly consistent upward shift in change rate between the 1980s and the 1990s, as shown in the final column. The only ones not to share in this trend were Birmingham (slight reduction in rate) and Newcastle (no change). By contrast, London's growth rate rose by almost 7 percentage points between the two decades, and Manchester, Glasgow, Leeds and Sheffield also experienced substantial positive shifts in rate.

Moreover, according to official population estimates, this upward trajectory has continued beyond 2001 for most cities, although not for London. As shown in Figure 2.1, all six principal cities of the English metropolitan counties registered an upward shift in average annual growth rate in the three years from 2001 compared with the preceding three years, with especially large rises for Liverpool, Manchester and Newcastle. As a result, all six are estimated to have gained population between 2001 and 2004, whereas only two were achieving this previously. By contrast, London's growth rate dropped back substantially between the two periods, although still growing in 2001-04 more strongly than all the other cities bar Manchester.

Table 2.1: Population change, for eight major cities (1981-2001)

City (administrative area)	2001 population (000s)	1981-91 change (%)	1991-2001 change (%)	Shift in change rate (% point)
London	7,322.4	0.4	7.2	6.9
Birmingham	984.6	-1.6	-2.0	-0.4
Glasgow	578.7	-11.7	-8.0	3.7
Leeds	715.6	-1.6	1.3	2.8
Liverpool	441.9	-8.0	-7.1	0.9
Manchester	422.9	-6.5	-2.3	4.2
Newcastle upon Tyne	266.2	-3.2	-3.2	0.0
Sheffield	513.1	-5.1	-1.3	3.7

Note: Figures rounded after calculation, so those on the shift in change rate between the two decades may not sum exactly.

Source: Calculated from revised mid-year estimates provided by the Office for National Statistics (ONS) and GRO-Scotland. Crown copyright

Figure 2.1: Population change, for seven major cities (1998-2001 and 2001-04) (% per year)

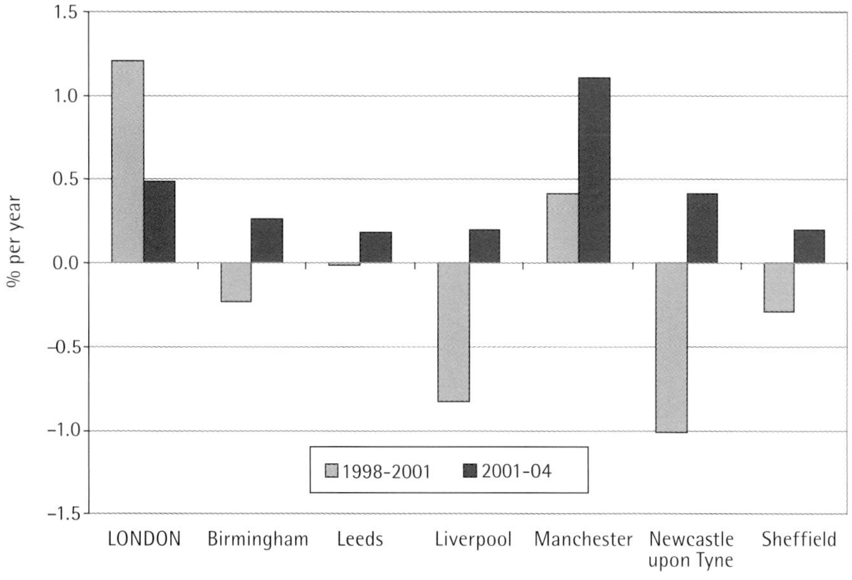

Note: Based on administrative areas (Greater London and six unitary authorities).

Source: Calculated from revised mid-year estimates provided by ONS. Crown copyright

To some extent, the post-2001 pattern may be due to the stage reached in the economic cycle as the growth 'ripple' moved outwards from South East England. On the other hand, there are developments taking place in these cities that do suggest a more sustained population revival. Perhaps most conspicuous among these is the return of residents to the more central parts of these cities. While London has led the field in this respect since its urban gentrification got underway in the 1960s, regional cities have been witnessing a growing interest in city centre living in recent years. According to case studies by the Institute for Public Policy Research (IPPR) (Nathan and Urwin, 2006, p 18), the city centre population of Manchester almost trebled between 1991 and 2001, Dundee's almost doubled and Liverpool's also rose by several thousand people. While students, graduates and other young adults were found to have dominated the repopulation of these three city centres up till now, the latest proposals for these cities are aiming to broaden the appeal of these areas so as to include larger numbers of retired people and families with children.

The role of within-UK migration

An overall population change such as that seen in these cities is the result of two components: natural increase (the surplus of births over deaths), and the net migration balance resulting from the combined effects of both within-country and international movements. As mentioned in Chapter 1, when this closer look is taken at such direct explanations (or 'proximate causes') of the urban population recovery, it would seem that there has been little alteration in patterns of within-UK migration as they affect the larger cities. Instead, it is found that trends in international migration provide the main key to understanding the upward shift in the growth rates of larger cities in recent years, together with a more selective role for natural increase.

Several lines of evidence can be drawn on to illustrate these points. Table 2.2 shows the upward shifts in overall population growth for London and the aggregate of the six metropolitan cities of England between 1991-97 and 1997-2004, and breaks these down into their natural increase and migration components. In both cases, it is natural increase that has been the main driver of population growth, but it was the migration component that was largely or wholly responsible for the rise in overall growth. In the case of London, while natural increase did accelerate between the two periods, the switch from overall migration loss to gain contributed almost three quarters of the capital's increased growth rate. As regards the six metropolitan cities, the halving of the rate of net migration loss between the two periods accounted for the entire upward shift in overall population growth because their natural increase weakened.

Table 2.2: Population change and its components, for London and six metropolitan cities (1991-2004) (% per year)

	Population change		Natural increase		Migration and other change	
	1991-97	1997-2004	1991-97	1997-2004	1991-97	1997-2004
London	0.43	0.77	0.52	0.61	–0.09	0.16
Mets	-0.19	-0.07	0.21	0.13	-0.40	-0.20

Note: Cities are defined on the best fit of unitary and district local authorities to primary urban areas (PUAs). Mets = metropolitan cities.

Source: Calculated from revised mid-year estimates provided by ONS. Crown copyright

Figure 2.2: Net out-migration from metropolitan England to the rest of the UK (1991-2004)

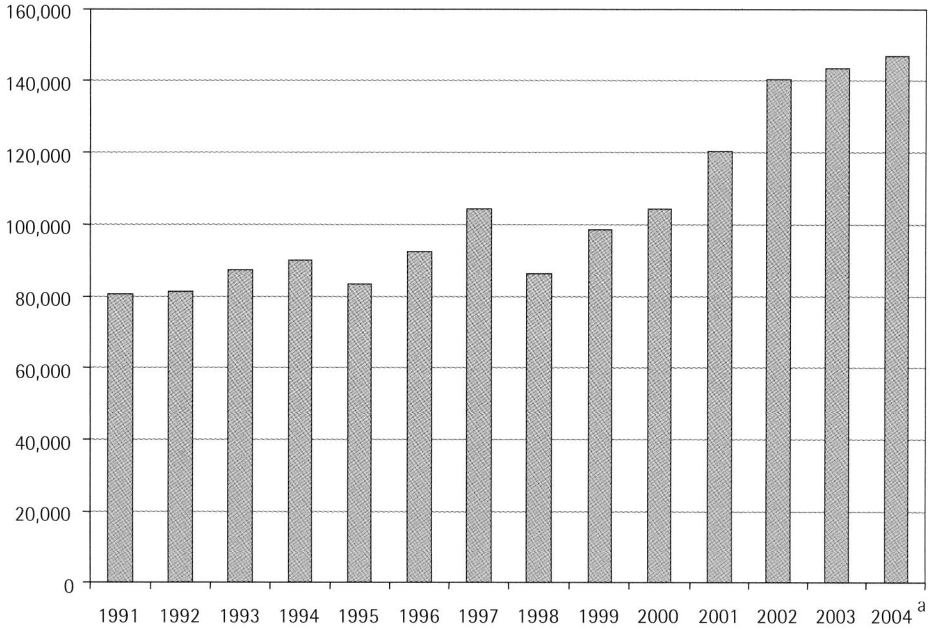

Note: Metropolitan England refers to Greater London and the six former metropolitan counties.
[a] 2004 relates to the 12 months ending June 2004, otherwise, calendar year.
Source: Data provided by ONS from the NHS Central Register. Crown copyright

The evidence that the upward shift in migration balance for larger cities was not primarily due to a reduction in their migration losses to the rest of the UK is provided in Figure 2.2. It is clear that there has been no long-term reduction in the net exodus of people from Greater London and the six English metropolitan counties since the early 1990s. Indeed, in the past few years there has been a marked acceleration in this process, to the extent that its recent levels of over 140,000 exceed that of any year since the continuous monitoring of sub-regional migration began in 1975 (see also Champion, 2005).

Figure 2.3 reveals how this metropolitan exodus impacts on the rest of England for 2003-04, the latest year for which data is available at the time of writing. In both halves of the country, there is a clear 'counter-urbanisation' gradient in the population change effect of within-UK migration. The latter becomes more positive as one moves down the settlement size ladder, with the rate shifting progressively further to the right from the largest settlement type through to the 'small towns and rural' type. The gradient across the settlement types is especially steep in the South and East, primarily owing to the massive net exodus from London. Meanwhile, in both broad regions, it is the small towns and rural type that is the main gainer through migration exchanges with the rest of the UK, with that in the North and West gaining at a rate not far short of its equivalent in the South and East.

Figure 2.3 also shows how these types of places were affected by the migration exchanges taking place with the rest of the world beyond the UK's borders. The overall picture is broadly the inverse of that for the within-UK migration, with its impact becoming less positive with reducing settlement size. As a result, for the larger cities in both halves of England, this international migration goes a long way to offsetting the within-UK migration losses. Indeed, in this particular year 2003-04, the six metropolitan cities of North and West England recorded an overall migration gain as a result of their immigration surplus exceeding their aggregate net loss of people to the rest of the UK.

Figure 2.3: Rates of within-UK and international net migration, for England, by settlement types (2003-04)

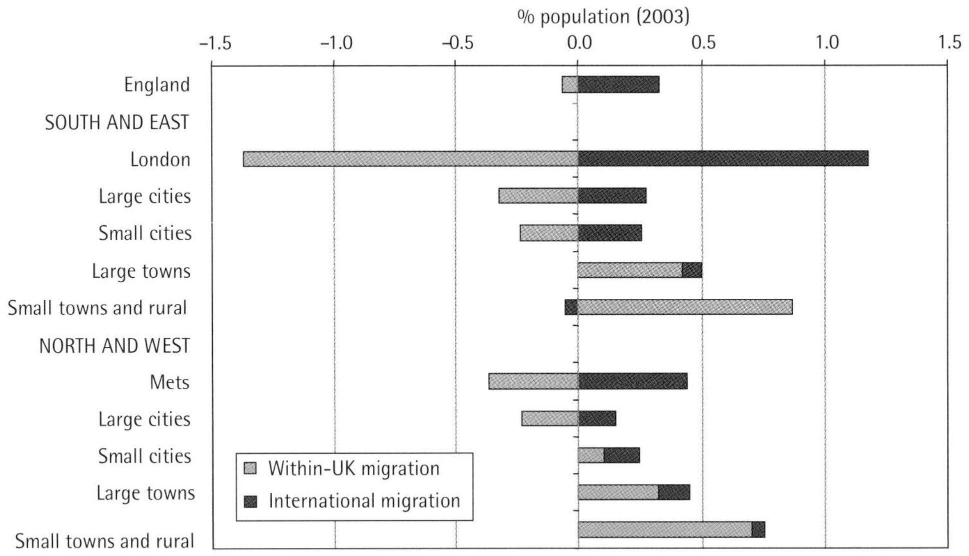

Note: Cities are defined on the best fit of unitary and district local authorities to PUAs (see Chapter 3).
Source: Calculated from revised mid-year estimates and data on components of change provided by ONS. Crown copyright

Unfortunately, there is no published data on international migration available on the same basis as this for before 2001, so it is impossible to chart the exact role that it has played in the long-term population recovery of urban England. From the evidence of Figure 2.3, however, net immigration from overseas has clearly been playing a very positive role in the population growth of the larger cities in recent years, whereas the larger cities are continuing to lose out substantially through their migration exchanges with other parts of the country. Hence the importance of a closer look at the composition of these within-UK migration flows in order to see whether the net exodus from the larger cities continues to be skewed towards the wealthier and more skilled elements of the population. Of course, there is also a strong case for trying to examine how the balance of international migration has been affecting the social complexion of our cities. This possibility is, however, denied us by virtue of the fact that census data only covers a country's own residents and so cannot provide any information about the considerable numbers of people who leave the UK each year.

3

The within-UK migration exchanges of the 27 large cities

This chapter introduces the 27 cities selected for the study and then uses the migration data from the 2001 Census to examine their migration exchanges with the rest of the UK. Its primary aim is to examine the occupational complexion of these exchanges in order to see whether or not the previous inability of British cities to retain and attract more higher skill people than others has continued through into the new century. Initially the 27 cities are treated as a single aggregate, but when we come to look at the social aspects of the migration flows, we also look at the cities individually. We show that it is especially important to distinguish London from the others, not just because of its much greater size but also because of its distinctive patterns. Once we do this, we find less of a shift from the picture previously derived from the 1991 and 1981 Censuses than our aggregate analysis suggests.

The cities

The cities covered in this study are identified in Map 3.1. The full rationale for selecting them is presented in Appendix B, but in brief they comprise the 27 largest cities that are also the principal cities of the 'city regions' of Great Britain identified by Coombes (2002). The latter criterion was adopted in order to have a ready-made basis for distinguishing the migration flows taking place between a city and its surrounding area, on the one hand, from its longer-distance exchanges with the rest of the UK, on the other – an aspect of the research that is taken up in Chapters 4 and 5. A city size cut-off of 195,000 residents was used; this was lower than a more 'natural' level of 200,000 because it was thought interesting to include Norwich that does not have the same industrial inheritance as most larger cities.

The cities are defined on the basis of their continuously built-up areas (note that in the census these are termed 'urban areas' in England and Wales, 'localities' in Scotland). These areas have very precise delineations on the ground that have been developed from the 2001 Census output areas. For the purposes of this study, however, we adopt a best fit of district and unitary local government areas to these (see Appendix B for the list of constituent areas for each city). This is to allow the use of the district-level special migration statistics (SMS) with their fuller coverage of the characteristics of migrants and their lesser degree of data perturbation caused by the disclosure control methods (see Appendix A).

In total, these 27 cities were home to 23.3 million people in 2001 and comprised around two in five of the total UK population of 58.8 million. London's urban area contained almost 8.3 million residents, making it well over three times the size of second-placed

Birmingham (2.3 million) and nearly 50 times the size of Norwich. Indeed, London accounts for over one third of the 27-city total and will obviously tend to dominate the latter. Later in this chapter we will demonstrate the importance of separating out the capital from the other 26 cities. First of all, however, we examine the aggregate picture.

Migration by age for the 27 cities combined

How did 'large-city Britain', as defined for the purposes of this study, fare in terms of its migration exchanges with the rest of the UK? Here we sum the statistics for the 27 cities, looking first at all people and then examining the patterns by age. The migration figures

Map 3.1: The 27 large cities and their city regions

presented here are restricted to people moving from known origins within the UK, thus excluding people who had been living outside the UK one year before the census and also those who ticked the box on the census form indicating that they had no usual address then (see Appendix A).

As shown in the final column of Table 3.1, in the 12 months before the census these 27 cities combined recorded inflows from the rest of the UK (including the other 26 cities) totalling almost 605,000 people and outflows totalling nearly 668,000. As a result, large-city Britain recorded an overall net loss of almost 63,000 to the rest of the UK. In terms of their total number of residents, the latter is equivalent to a loss of 0.27% in this one year (that is, a reduction in population of 2.7% if this pattern was repeated across a full decade). Another way of portraying this pattern is to say that there were just over nine people moving to these 27 cities for every 10 people leaving them, as shown by the in/out ratio of 0.906 in the last row in the table.

Table 3.1: Migration for 27 large cities combined, total and by age (2000-01)

Measure	0-15	16-19	20-24	25-44	45+	All ages
Residents	4,744,075	1,187,110	1,661,846	7,256,380	8,488,832	23,338,243
Inflows	59,119	92,210	176,296	218,878	58,348	604,851
Outflows	97,161	54,433	142,056	268,115	105,954	667,719
Net flow	-38,042	37,777	34,240	-49,237	-47,606	-62,868
Inflow rate	1.25	7.77	10.61	3.02	0.69	2.59
Outflow rate	2.05	4.59	8.55	3.69	1.25	2.86
Net flow rate	-0.80	3.18	2.06	-0.68	-0.56	-0.27
In/out ratio	0.608	1.694	1.241	0.816	0.551	0.906

Note: Rate is the flow count as % of number of residents at the 2001 Census. In/out ratio is calculated by dividing the inflows by the outflows.

Source: Calculated from the 2001 Census SMS, Table MG101. Crown copyright

Table 3.1 also provides the same measures by age, based on groups that represent life stages associated with particular migration behaviour. Very clear differences are evident between these broad ages. For the under-16s and those aged 25-44 and 45+, there was overall net migration loss to the rest of the UK and, as shown by the net flow rate, this represents around 0.6-0.8% of the cities' numbers in these age groups. By contrast, there were strong net inflows of 16-19s and 20-24s, adding to their numbers at the rate of 2-3% for this one-year period. As measured by the in/out ratio, nearly 17 people aged 16-19 moved into these 27 cities for every 10 leaving them, while at the other extreme the ratios for the under 16s and those aged 45+ indicate that only around six were arriving there for every 10 exiting them.

These patterns will come as no surprise to those who monitor age-specific migration patterns. The inflow to cities of young adults and the departure of older people, including retirees and parents with school-age children, are well-established features of migration not only in the UK but worldwide. In the 2001 Census, they appear even clearer than in previous enumerations because of this being the first time that students moving to attend university/college and graduates leaving there have been treated as migrants. This change in definitions makes it problematic to gauge the scale of difference from previous experience, but these results from the 2001 Census are consistent with the picture conveyed by the NHS Central Register data for Metropolitan England (see Figure 2.2). Overall, Britain's larger cities are, in aggregate, still suffering a substantial loss of people through their migration exchanges with the rest of the UK.

Taking a life course perspective on this pre-census year of migration, it can be seen as encouraging for the cities that the net loss of 38,000 under-16s is almost entirely offset by the net influx of 16- to 19-year-olds. Set against this, however, is the observation from Table 3.1 that the cities' overall net gain of 0- to 24-year-olds (around 34,000) is of relatively short-term benefit to them, given the absolute volume of their net losses of people aged 25 and over. The overall picture for large-city Britain is one of net out-migration across the majority of the working-age span and beyond.

Migration by skill level for the 27 cities combined

Against that background, we now look at the social composition of this migration. We do this on the basis of the National Statistics Socioeconomic Classification (NS-SEC), which in 2001 replaced the SEG (Socioeconomic Group) system used in previous censuses. The new classification is more strongly based on the skill and qualification levels of jobs and so is better attuned to our concerns over human capital than the SEG's central split between manual and non-manual work.

We take advantage of this development by grouping the NS-SEC's eight occupational categories (see Appendix A) into four skill levels, as follows:

- 'Higher managerial and professional' (including large employers: NS-SEC 1.1 and 1.2)
- 'Lower managerial and professional' (NS-SEC 2)
- 'Intermediate' (including small employers and own account workers: NS-SEC 3 and 4)
- 'Low' (comprising lower supervisory and technical, semi-routine and routine occupations: NS-SEC 5, 6 and 7).

In addition, there are certain people who have not been allocated an occupation, either because they lay outside the age span 16-74 (the only ages for which occupation was coded by the 2001 Census) or for other reasons. For present purposes, we have put these into two further groups – 'Full-time students' and 'Others' – but our primary focus for the purposes of this study is on the four skill levels.

At this stage, it is important to be clear about which sorts of people we are looking at and those that we have to omit. The data that it is necessary for us to use for this analysis (from Table MG109 – see Appendix A) is based on a migration concept developed specially for the 2001 Census's origin/destination statistics, namely the moving group. This refers to either one person moving on their own or two or more people who had been living at the same previous address before moving together into a private household. Moving groups are classified on the basis of the NS-SEC of their 'reference person', so we do not know the NS-SEC of any other people that they may contain.

A further challenge is posed by the fact that there is no obvious denominator that we can use to calculate rates of migration. Moving groups, by definition, can be found only in the migrant population: there is no equivalent in the rest of the population to act as the 'population at risk' (of moving in the pre-census year). Rather than using the total number of households or residents as a proxy for this, we do not attempt to use rates but instead have opted to rely on the in/out ratio. As already seen from Table 3.1, this measure gives a clear indication of the relative attractiveness of cities for the different groups in the population by showing how balanced or one-way their inflows and outflows are.

The results of applying this approach to the within-UK flows of the 27 cities combined are presented in Table 3.2. The total inflows and outflows of moving group reference persons (MGRPs) indicate a more even balance between the two than the equivalent figure for all people seen above: an in/out ratio of 0.976 as opposed to that of 0.906 shown in Table

3.1. This arises largely from the smaller average size of moving groups arriving in the cities compared with those leaving them and is associated especially with the strong city-ward flow of people who were 'Full-time students' at the census. Almost all of these will have been moving out of their parental home to university on their own, that is, as one-person moving groups. Far more of these were moving to term-time addresses in these cities than were leaving parental homes to take up a university place in one of the other cities or elsewhere in the UK. Their ratio of 1.676, signifying five arriving to become 'Full-time students' in these cities for every three leaving their home city for this purpose, is almost identical to the ratio for 16- to 19-year-olds shown in Table 3.1. By contrast, for the 'Other' category, the ratio signifies only two arrivals in these cities for every three departures. This reflects to a degree the ratio seen for older people in Table 3.1 but no doubt is also affected by the return from university of those graduates who were still looking for work at the time of the census the following spring and were therefore not classifiable by occupation.

Table 3.2: Within-UK migration, of MGRPs classified by NS-SEC at the census, for 27 cities combined (2000-01)

NS-SEC of MGRPs at the census	Inflows	Outflows	In/out ratio
All MGRPs	389,902	399,368	0.976
Full-time students	76,318	45,527	1.676
Other unclassified MGRPs	31,331	45,472	0.689
All occupationally classified MGRPs	282,253	308,369	0.915
Higher managerial and professional	67,162	69,515	0.966
Lower managerial and professional	99,404	106,289	0.935
Intermediate	54,210	60,828	0.891
Low	61,477	71,739	0.857

Source: Calculated from the 2001 Census SMS, Table MG109. Crown copyright

Turning to the occupationally classified MGRPs in Table 3.2, it can be seen that their overall in/out ratio is, at 0.915, quite similar to that for all people (0.906, from Table 3.1). Our main interest, however, concerns how the ratio varies across the four skill levels and, in particular, whether the in/out ratio is lower for the high skill groups, as was found in research on earlier censuses. In fact, there is a clear gradient in in/out ratio across these four groups, but the relationship is the opposite of that observed previously, with the ratio declining regularly with skill level. The number of MGRPs who moved into these cities and were classified in highest status group of Higher managerial and professional was almost as high as the number moving out of these cities and classified this way on census night. At the other extreme, for those in the 'Low skill' category, only about six moved to these cities for every seven moving out of them.

Migration by skill level for the 27 cities individually

Does this apparent reversal in the relationship between migration and skill level for large cities since 1990-91 reflect a systemic change in migration patterns in Britain, associated with the rejuvenation of the cities as places to work and live in? Alternatively, could the observed shift be the result of cyclical factors, such that cities are more attractive to higher skill people in a period of economic boom like that existing in the year before the 2001 Census than in a period of economic recession like 1990-91? Or is the shift merely an artefact of the differences of methodology between the present study and previous research? Breaking down the aggregate picture – even just separating out London from the other 26 cities – goes a long way towards answering these questions.

As mentioned earlier, one of the main changes from the previous work by Champion and Fisher (2003) is that the present study covers a much larger range of city sizes, so a first step is to gauge whether the inclusion of non-conurbation cities can explain the different patterns of 2000-01. We approach this test of the significance of city size in two stages. First, in Figure 3.1 we chart the overall in/out ratio for all classified MGRPs for cities arranged in descending size order. Then, in Table 3.3, for each of the 27 cities (again arranged in descending size order), we rank the four skill levels on the basis of their in/out ratio.

Figure 3.1: In/out ratios for all classified MGRPs, for 27 cities arranged by urban area population size

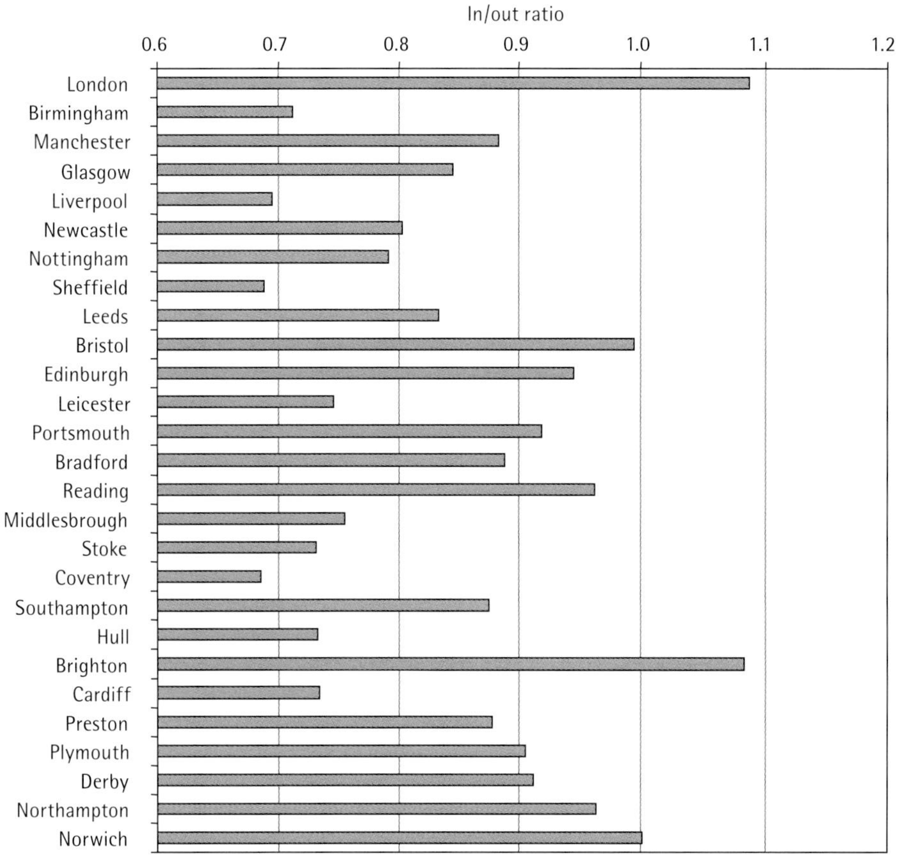

Source: Calculated from the 2001 Census SMS, Table MG109. Crown copyright

The in/out ratios for all classified MGRPs (Figure 3.1) exhibit no clear relationship with city size. The four cities with the highest ratios are well scattered across the size spectrum, including London and Norwich at the two extremes and Bristol and Brighton at ranks 10 and 21 respectively. Moreover, while it is the case that the nine largest cities after London all display ratios that are well below unity, there are proportionately as many with ratios as low as those of Birmingham, Liverpool and Sheffield amongst the remaining two thirds of cases. In particular, Leicester, Middlesbrough, Stoke, Coventry, Hull and Cardiff all have ratios of 0.75 or below, signifying no more than three occupationally classified MGRPs moving in for every four moving out.

In terms of the relative positions of the four skill groups' in/out ratios (see the right-hand four columns of Table 3.3), the most notable feature is how few of the 27 cities share exactly the same relationship as the 27-city aggregate seen in Table 3.2. London and

Manchester are the only cases where there is a regular decline in in/out ratio with skill level (signified by their 1-2-3-4 listing of ranks). Indeed, including these two, there are only four cities where the highest ratio is for the 'Higher managerial and professional' group (indicated by rank 1 in the 'Higher M&P' column). By contrast, for a much larger number of cities – 11 in all – this skill level appears to be the hardest of the four to attract and retain (indicated by rank 4 in the 'Higher M&P' column). Moreover, there is a clear progression across the four skill levels in the majority of these cases, with the higher attraction/retention at each step down the skills ladder (signified by their 4-3-2-1 listing of ranks). This applies to Newcastle, Nottingham, Sheffield, Leicester, Portsmouth, Middlesbrough, Coventry and Hull.

Table 3.3: In/out ratios for skill groups, and ranking of skill groups, for 27 cities arranged by Urban Area population size

	In/out ratio				Ranking of skill group (1=high)			
City (arranged by size)	Higher M&P	Lower M&P	Inter-mediate	Low skill	Higher M&P	Lower M&P	Inter-mediate	Low skill
London	1.336	1.218	0.996	0.713	1	2	3	4
Birmingham	0.697	0.677	0.676	0.807	2	3	4	1
Manchester	0.927	0.881	0.876	0.848	1	2	3	4
Glasgow	0.819	0.818	0.877	0.882	3	4	2	1
Liverpool	0.694	0.665	0.648	0.769	2	3	4	1
Newcastle	0.730	0.757	0.822	0.911	4	3	2	1
Nottingham	0.612	0.786	0.811	0.985	4	3	2	1
Sheffield	0.606	0.630	0.702	0.845	4	3	2	1
Leeds	0.845	0.797	0.872	0.841	2	4	1	3
Bristol	0.967	0.972	1.069	1.001	4	3	1	2
Edinburgh	0.930	0.891	1.047	0.967	3	4	1	2
Leicester	0.623	0.667	0.818	0.908	4	3	2	1
Portsmouth	0.809	0.854	0.953	1.084	4	3	2	1
Bradford	0.776	0.834	0.819	1.099	4	2	3	1
Reading	1.028	0.970	0.983	0.826	1	3	2	4
Middlesbrough	0.619	0.749	0.764	0.835	4	3	2	1
Stoke	0.588	0.717	0.609	0.933	4	2	3	1
Coventry	0.500	0.627	0.719	0.961	4	3	2	1
Southampton	0.858	0.881	0.748	1.006	3	2	4	1
Hull	0.557	0.613	0.624	1.020	4	3	2	1
Brighton	1.067	1.148	1.093	0.992	3	1	2	4
Cardiff	0.752	0.699	0.817	0.705	2	4	1	3
Preston	0.831	0.770	0.878	1.085	3	4	2	1
Plymouth	0.822	0.743	0.910	1.163	3	4	2	1
Derby	1.031	0.842	0.822	0.975	1	3	4	2
Northampton	1.020	0.928	1.068	0.910	2	3	1	4
Norwich	0.938	0.953	0.909	1.187	3	2	4	1

Note: M&P = managerial and professional.

Source: Calculated from the 2001 Census SMS, Table MG109. Crown copyright

This evidence suggests that the inclusion of non-conurbation cities in the present study plays no part in explaining why the relationship between in/out ratio and skill level shown by the 27-city aggregate for 2000-01 is different from that found previously. By looking at the 27 cities individually, it has become clear that the majority pattern remains the one that was shown from the 1981 and 1991 Census data, despite our study including smaller cities that from the counter-urbanisation literature might have been expected to be more attractive as places to live.

What is much clearer in 2001 than from previous censuses, however, is London's distinctiveness and the scale of its contribution to the overall 27-city aggregate. If the capital is omitted, the aggregate relationship between in/out ratio and skill level switches to negative. As shown in Table 3.4, the in/out ratio for the 26 other cities combined is highest for the 'Low skill' category and declines up the skills ladder – very similar to the general pattern for the eight conurbations studied by Champion and Fisher (2003). A particularly impressive feature of Table 3.4 is the fact that London accounts for over two fifths of the total inflows of managerial and professional MGRPs to the 27 cities, while contributing less than a quarter of their total inflows of the 'Low skill' category.

Table 3.4: Within-UK migration, all MGRPs classified by skill level at the census, for London and for the other 26 cities combined (2000-01)

Skill level of MGRPs at the census	Inflows	Outflows	In/out ratio
London			
All occupationally classified MGRPs	103,141	94,863	1.087
Higher managerial and professional	28,355	21,221	1.336
Lower managerial and professional	40,499	33,758	1.218
Intermediate	19,364	19,448	0.996
Low	14,923	20,936	0.713
Other 26 cities			
All occupationally classified MGRPs	179,112	213,506	0.839
Higher managerial and professional	38,807	48,294	0.804
Lower managerial and professional	58,905	73,029	0.807
Intermediate	34,846	41,380	0.842
Low	46,554	50,803	0.916

Source: Calculated from the 2001 Census SMS, Table MG109. Crown copyright

Figure 3.2 reinforces this point about the distinctiveness of London by separating out the five largest cities besides London (Birmingham, Manchester, Glasgow, Liverpool and Newcastle) from the remaining 21 cities. For these five cities combined, the relationship between migration ratio and skill level bears a much closer resemblance to the aggregate of the remaining 21 than it does to London's pattern. Their only differences from the 21-city aggregate are their lower in/out ratios for all four skill levels, comparing like with like, and their 'Higher managerial and professional's' ratio not being the lowest of the four skill levels, this latter being entirely due to Manchester being more like London than the modal pattern (as seen above from Table 3.3).

Figure 3.2: In/out ratio for MGRPs, by skill level, for 27 cities grouped by urban area population size

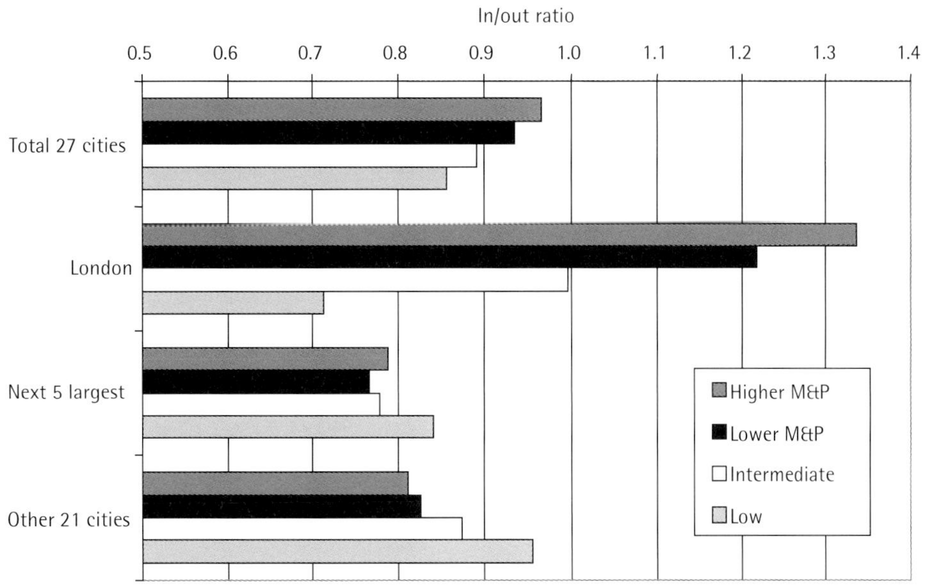

Source: Calculated from the 2001 Census SMS, Table MG109. Crown copyright

We now move on to probe how the patterns observed in this chapter have arisen. An important first step is to distinguish between the two main components of these cities' migration exchanges with the rest of the UK. In the next chapter, we describe and analyse the longer-distance exchanges that normally represent the movement of human capital away from the sphere of influence of one city and into that of another. Then, in Chapter 5 we look at the more local flows between the cities and their surrounding areas that can be seen as primarily a process of residential sorting within the wider city region.

4

The longer-distance movement of human capital

This chapter focuses on the longer-distance component of the 27 cities' migration exchanges. As such, here we are dealing with the 'exchange of human capital' between places. For instance, when a person moves away from a city to another part of the country lying beyond the immediate sphere of influence of that city, this will normally constitute a loss to the labour force available to that city and thereby weaken its economic base, and vice versa in terms of a person moving to the city from another part of the country.

Particular attention is given to the migration of the most skilled element of the workforce, namely those in 'Higher managerial and professional' occupations. While a ready supply of people prepared to work in low paid jobs can help to facilitate economic expansion, it is now widely accepted in both academic and policy circles that the rise of the 'knowledge-based economy' plays a crucial role in successful economic regeneration (for example, HM Treasury et al, 2006). A key challenge for cities, therefore, is how far they can develop the innovative and creative industries that form a major part of this sector's growth and, related to this, how they can do better in attracting and retaining the high quality human capital on which these industries depend (Florida, 2002; Simmie, 2004).

Given the focus on the qualitative dimensions of this migration, the analysis in this chapter is based entirely on data relating to the socioeconomic classification of migrants. As seen in Chapter 3, this means using the counts of MGRPs, with these being assigned to one of six categories – four occupationally classified 'skill groups', 'Full-time students' and a residual group. We begin by looking at the aggregate performance of large-city Britain across these six categories, before examining the experience of the 27 cities individually in terms of their in/out ratios for the four skill groups. Then, in order to get an insight into what may be affecting their differential performance, a four-way split of the cities is used as the basis for comparing the characteristics of those that we find to be more and less successful in attracting and retaining high skill people. Finally, we investigate the rather distinctive role that London plays in the longer-distance migration exchanges of the other 26 cities.

The aggregate picture

The overall performance of large-city Britain in relation to the longer-distance component of its migration exchanges with the rest of the UK is shown in Table 4.1. This adopts the same basis as was used in Table 3.2 to show the cities' total migration exchanges with the rest of the UK (including with the rest of their city regions), and the in/out ratios from that table are included here in the final column for comparative purposes. What this shows is that the two sets of in/out ratios are rather similar to each other, but this is not altogether surprising because these longer-distance exchanges account for the majority of the cities' total migration exchanges. The 296,408 MGRPs recorded as arriving in these 27 cities from beyond their city region boundaries form 76% of the total 389,902 in-migrant MGRPs, while the 288,648 MGRPs moving out of these cities to beyond their city region boundaries comprise 72% of their total outflows to the rest of the UK. In other words, only around one quarter of the 27 cities' migration exchanges is with the rest of their city regions, this component being the topic of Chapter 5.

Table 4.1: Longer-distance migration exchanges of MGRPs classified by NS-SEC at the census, for 27 cities combined (2000-01)

NS-SEC of MGRPs at the census	Inflows	Outflows	In/out ratio	In/out ratio for all UK
All MGRPs	296,408	288,648	1.027	0.976
Full-time students	65,855	39,885	1.651	1.676
Other unclassified MGRPs	22,801	30,952	0.737	0.689
All occupationally classified MGRPs	207,752	217,811	0.954	0.915
Higher managerial and professional	53,119	53,231	0.998	0.966
Lower managerial and professional	74,259	76,122	0.976	0.935
Intermediate	38,496	41,381	0.930	0.891
Low	41,878	47,077	0.890	0.857

Source: Calculated from the 2001 Census SMS, Table MG109. Crown copyright

Table 4.1 shows that the balance of inflows to outflows arising from this longer-distance migration is more favourable to large-city Britain than are the overall exchanges with the whole of the UK including the rest of their city regions (compare the last two columns of the table). In terms of all MGRPs, the longer-distance inflows outnumber the outflows by some 8,000, translating into an in/out ratio of 1.027. This is as much above unity as the ratio for the overall exchanges was below unity. All four occupationally classified categories display a higher in/out ratio, and thus more positive balance, for longer-distance migration than when the more local exchanges are included. The same is true of the 'Other' unclassified category. 'Full-time students' provide the exception, but their 1.651 ratio still indicates a strong city-ward movement of this group.

Even so, we are faced with a broad pattern of longer-distance migration for large-city Britain that is quite similar to that for its total within-UK exchanges as described in Chapter 3. It is one that involves a substantial net gain of students, whereby there are more people arriving in these 27 cities from outside their city regions for the purposes of study than people leaving these cities in order to study elsewhere in the UK beyond their city regions. It is also one in which the MGRPs, who at the time of the census could not be classified by occupation for any other reason (such as being long-term unemployed, having never had a job or being aged 75 or over), were much more likely to be leaving the city than arriving there. Finally, there is the same positive and regular relationship between in/out ratio and skill level, with the inflows and outflows of the highest skill group being virtually in balance at one extreme and with 11% fewer 'Low skill' arrivals than departures at the other. Thus, analysis of this set of migration flows will provide a large part of the explanation for the overall patterns described in Chapter 3.

The 27 cities individually

Before moving towards a more formal attempt at explaining this picture, we look at the individual experiences of the 27 cities so as to get a better idea of the extent of variation between them and to provide an insight into the types of factors that might help to explain why some cities appear more attractive to high quality human capital than others. We start by comparing the cities on the basis of their in/out ratios for all MGRPs, then examine how much they differ in terms of the migration of 'Full-time students' and then turn to the occupationally classified segment and the question of the extent to which these cities' longer-distance exchanges share the positive relationship between ratio and skill level that has been observed for large-city Britain in aggregate. As in Chapter 3, we assess whether there is a city size factor at work, by arranging cities on the basis of urban area population size.

Figure 4.1 shows the migration balance for all MGRPs. Despite the 27 city aggregate recording the net gain seen above, only nine of the cities display in/out ratios in excess of 1.0. That these two observations are compatible is due to the fact that the majority of these nine cities are larger ones, not least London but also Nottingham, Sheffield, Leeds, Bristol, Edinburgh and Portsmouth, the latter being the median city in terms of size. Two thirds of the cities thus received fewer MGRPs from beyond their city regions than they dispatched thence in the pre-census year. Liverpool appears least attractive on this measure, with barely seven arrivals for every 10 departures, but Birmingham, Leicester, Middlesbrough, Stoke and Hull also have ratios of only around eight arrivals for every 10 departures.

Figure 4.1: In/out ratio for 27 cities' migration exchanges beyond their city regions: all MGRPs

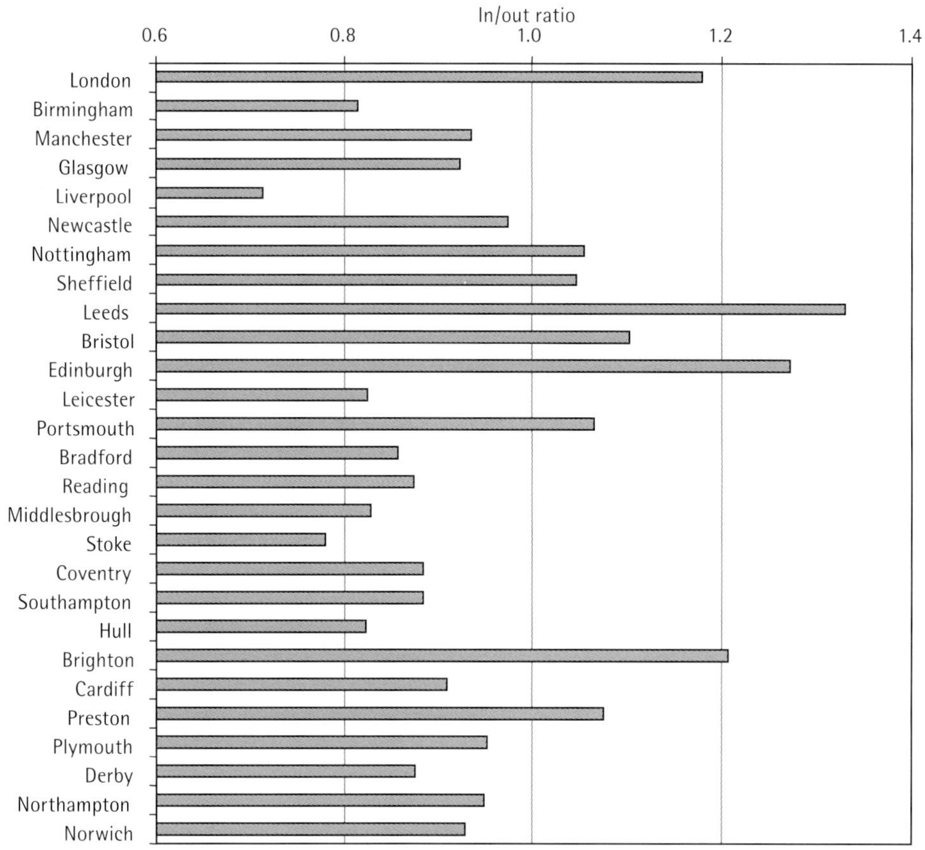

Source: Calculated from the 2001 Census SMS, Table MG109. Crown copyright

As we have seen, a key element in the dynamism of these cities is their overall net gain of people who were in full-time study at the time of the census. This is amply confirmed by Figure 4.2, which shows that virtually all of the 27 cities shared this experience. Only five of them received fewer 'Full-time students' from beyond their city region boundary in the year before the census than they saw departing for their studies in the opposite direction – Bradford, Reading, Middlesbrough, Derby and Northampton. At the other extreme, 10 cities gained two or more students from outside their regions for every one that they lost. In the case of Leeds, the ratio was over four to one, although – despite the undoubted importance of the universities there – the extremeness of this statistic probably arises from a difference in the type of first-year student accommodation available there or from some vagary in the way that students were treated in the census. Given that, by definition, MGRPs are identified only if they live in households and not in communal establishments, it seems likely that some universities either do not place many first-year students in halls of residence or else took a rather generous approach to recognising households in such accommodation. Nevertheless, any such quirks can hardly undermine the main point that the populations of large cities, with just a few exceptions, benefit from the movements taking place as a result of people entering higher education.

Figure 4.2: In/out ratio for 27 cities' migration exchanges beyond their city regions: 'Full-time students'

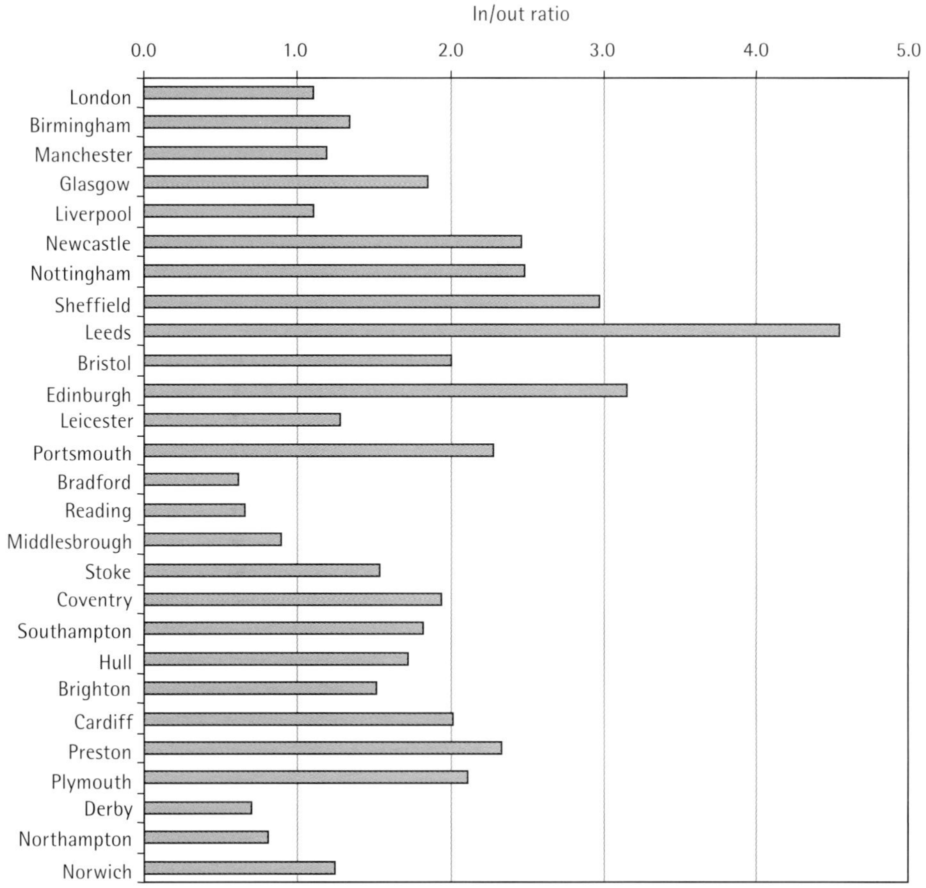

Source: Calculated from the 2001 Census SMS, Table MG109. Crown copyright

When we restrict attention to those MGRPs who could be classified by occupation at the time of the census, the picture for cities becomes less positive. In the first place, as shown in the first data column of Table 4.2, only three cities – London, Edinburgh and Brighton – received more people of this type from beyond their city regions than they sent out. At the other extreme, fewer than seven arrivals for every 10 departures were recorded by six cities, namely Liverpool, Newcastle, Sheffield, Stoke, Coventry and Hull.

The picture is similar for the 'Higher managerial and professional' category, except that the range of in/out ratios is larger (Table 4.2, second data column). In this case, four cities – London, Brighton, Derby and Northampton – received through longer-distance migration more MGRPs with this occupational classification at the census than they lost, although Edinburgh and Reading also come very close to this. London's performance in this respect, gaining more than 15 such people for every 10 lost, is even more outstanding than for

Table 4.2: In/out ratio for 27 cities' migration exchanges beyond their city regions: all classified, 'Higher managerial and professional', and four skill groups ranked

City (arranged by size)	In/out ratio for all classified MGRPs	In/out ratio for Higher M&P MGRPs	Ranking of skill group on in/out ratio (1 = highest)			
			Higher M&P	Lower M&P	Inter-mediate	Low skill
London	1.309	1.571	1	2	3	4
Birmingham	0.723	0.725	2	3	4	1
Manchester	0.912	0.957	1	2	4	3
Glasgow	0.812	0.718	4	3	2	1
Liverpool	0.620	0.639	2	3	4	1
Newcastle	0.699	0.672	2	4	3	1
Nottingham	0.783	0.605	4	3	2	1
Sheffield	0.653	0.584	4	3	2	1
Leeds	0.855	0.855	3	4	2	1
Bristol	0.985	0.948	4	3	1	2
Edinburgh	1.016	0.991	3	4	2	1
Leicester	0.702	0.628	3	4	2	1
Portsmouth	0.905	0.793	4	3	2	1
Bradford	0.897	0.777	4	3	2	1
Reading	0.922	0.985	1	2	3	4
Middlesbrough	0.757	0.621	4	2	3	1
Stoke	0.621	0.582	3	2	4	1
Coventry	0.643	0.487	4	3	2	1
Southampton	0.773	0.830	1	2	4	3
Hull	0.641	0.597	2	4	3	1
Brighton	1.195	1.132	3	1	2	4
Cardiff	0.705	0.710	3	4	2	1
Preston	0.852	0.809	3	4	2	1
Plymouth	0.738	0.717	2	4	3	1
Derby	0.896	1.103	1	3	4	2
Northampton	0.970	1.012	2	3	1	4
Norwich	0.843	0.840	2	3	4	1

Source: calculated from the 2001 Census SMS, Table MG109. Crown copyright

its ratio for all classified MGRPs. At the other extreme, Coventry recorded fewer than five arrivals from beyond its city region for every 10 moving in the opposite direction.

Looking across the four skill groups for each city, how common is the positive relationship between in/out ratio and skill level found for the 27 city aggregate in Table 4.1? Given what was found in Chapter 3 about the massive influence of London on the aggregate picture, it is perhaps not surprising to find that only two cities conform exactly to the aggregate pattern of a progressive decline in ratio with lower skill – London itself and Reading (signified by the 1-2-3-4 distribution across the four right-hand columns of Table 4.2). An additional three cities also have a higher in/out ratio for 'Higher managerial and professional' than for any of the other three skill levels (indicated by 1 in the 'Higher M&P' column), these being Manchester, Southampton and Derby.

At the other extreme, for a larger number of cities – eight in all – the 'Higher managerial and professional' group is the one that they are least successful in attracting and retaining. Moreover, in six of these cases, there is a regular progression of the ratio declining with each step up the skills ladder (signified by a 4-3-2-1 distribution across the ranking). These six are Glasgow, Nottingham, Sheffield, Portsmouth, Bradford and Coventry, and the other two with higher losses of this group than the other three skill levels are Bristol and Middlesbrough. The fact that these contrasts between cities often echo those in the previous chapter (as can be seen by comparing Tables 3.3 and 4.2) is largely due to the fact that flows analysed here make up about 75% of the flows in the earlier analysis.

Finally, for the vast majority of the cities, it is the 'Low skill' category that displays the highest in/out ratio. In most of these cases, it is therefore this category that comes closest to an even balance between inflows and outflows (rather than involving a ratio of over unity). This could be related to the traditional lack of longer-distance mobility of this group, but mobility levels of MGRPs cannot be calculated because there is no way of compiling a 'population at risk' from the 2001 Census data. The mechanism that generally drives longer-distance migration is labour market imbalance, and it may be that de-industrialisation and other processes have left few places with the need for major migrant inflows of this lower skill group.

Factors underlying variations between cities

In the results of the empirical analyses described above, patterns have begun to emerge in terms of their migration exchanges with areas beyond their city region boundaries and, especially, in relation to which cities seem to be more successful than others in attracting and retaining people. The main purpose of this section is to identify the city characteristics that are associated with this patterning, so as to obtain an insight into factors that may be aiding or obstructing the sorts of migration that can help in the process of urban regeneration. The literature on the determinants of migration (see Champion et al, 1998a) reveals a much larger number of factors than we have cities in our sample, so we adopt a classificatory approach to this question rather than using formal modelling techniques. This involves grouping our cities into types on the basis of their migration and then looking for differences between these types for a range of potential migration determinants.

For this purpose we have adopted a four-fold classification of the cities, as shown in Table 4.3. The methodology for this is described in Appendix C. In brief, the first step was to separate out cities with high levels of net immigration from outside the UK, because of the strong association that this tends to have with the level of net out-migration to the rest of the UK. London is the prime example of this (as seen above in Figure 2.3), but Brighton and Reading also had high rates of immigration around this time and can be labelled 'gateway' cities. The remaining 24 cities have been divided into three equal-sized groups on the basis of a summed ranking of three in/out ratios (all MGRPs, 'Higher managerial and professional' MGRPs, and 'Low skill' MGRPs), labelling them as 'stronger', 'moderate' and 'weaker'. For these, the analysis of characteristics is based on the seven English cities in each type owing to the difficulty of obtaining comparable data for the other countries.

Aggregating the data on longer-distance migration to these four types of cities (Figure 4.3) confirms how distinctive they are. On each of three migration measures shown, it is the gateway cities that display the highest in/out ratio, although for all MGRPs their aggregate ratio is only marginally higher than that of the stronger cities type. Then, as would be expected from the method used to classify the cities, the ratios fall as one moves from the

Table 4.3: Types of cities

Type	Cities in England	Other cities
Gateway	London, Reading, Brighton	
Stronger	Bristol, Preston, Portsmouth, Leeds, Norwich, Northampton, Derby	Edinburgh
Moderate	Manchester, Nottingham, Plymouth, Bradford, Newcastle, Southampton, Sheffield	Glasgow
Weaker	Coventry, Leicester, Birmingham, Hull, Middlesbrough, Liverpool, Stoke	Cardiff

Source: See Appendix C for details of the classification method

stronger type through the moderate cities to the weaker ones. The chart also confirms the distinction between the gateway cities and the others in terms of the relationship between the three migration measures. Whereas for the former the ratio is highest for the 'Higher managerial and professional' category and lowest for all MGRPs, for the other three city types the reverse is the case. As a result, the ratios for this high skill category span a wider range than for the other two measures, as previously noted from Table 4.2. All this means, however, is that any relationship found for the migration determinants across the city types will apply just as much to the high skill category as to their more general migration performance.

Figure 4.3: City types' in/out ratios with the UK beyond their city regions

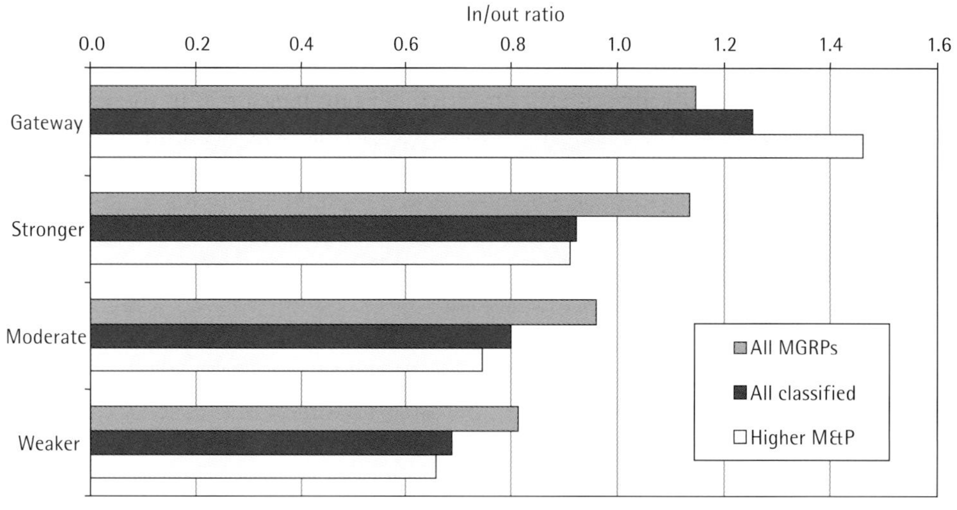

Source: Calculated from the 2001 Census SMS, Table MG109. Crown copyright

The most commonly cited determinants of longer-distance migration concern the labour market and the strength of local economy (Champion et al, 1998a). Six of the 33 characteristics that we tested for their relationship with migration performance were concerned with this. Figure 4.4 shows how each of our four city types scored relative to the national average on these six variables. A first glance at the overall patterns confirms the key role of the state of the labour market, as the bars generally get progressively shorter as the migration performance weakens. At the same time, it is worth comparing the general level of the labour market indicators against the national figure (shown as 1.0 line on the chart). All six are well below the latter for the weaker and moderate city types, and only a couple exceed it for the stronger cities, helping to account for the prevailing pattern of below-unity migration ratios shown for classified MGRPs for these three city types.

Figure 4.4: Performance of the city types on six labour market indicators relative to the national average

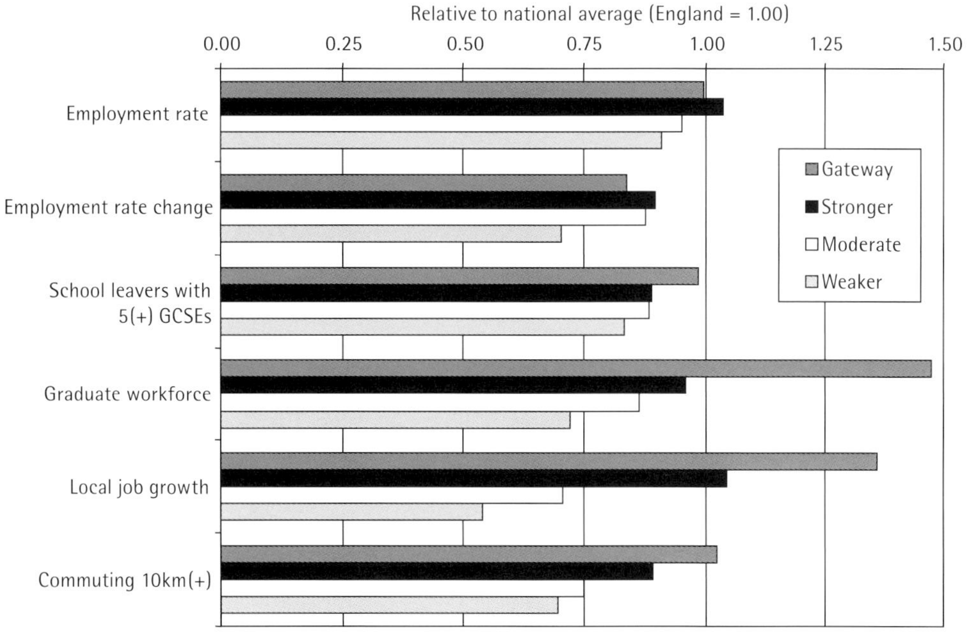

Note: See Appendix D for the full specification and source of the characteristics.

Turning to the differences across the four city types for the individual labour market characteristics (Figure 4.4), we look first at two employment rate measures. In the case of the rate itself (defined as the proportion of working-age people who were in work at the time of the 2001 Census), there is found to be a general relationship along the lines expected, namely with the higher rate being associated with the stronger migration performance. Only the gateway city type does not fit the relationship perfectly, because its employment rate is somewhat lower than for the stronger cities. The same applies to employment rate change (calculated for the decade 1991-2001).

The pattern is similar for the other four labour market characteristics, except that for these the relationship with migration performance applies right across the four city types (Figure 4.4). The gateway cities have the highest aggregate score for the educational achievement of school leavers, the proportion of graduates in the workforce, the rate of local job growth since 1991 and the proportion of the workforce commuting at least 10km. For each of these, the scores decline progressively down the ranking of city types; the gradient is least marked for educational achievement, whereas it is especially steep for graduate workforce and local job growth.

A summary of the same tests carried out using the other 27 potential migration determinants is presented in Table 4.4. As with the observations above on the relationships between relative migration performance and labour market factors, a key question to explore is whether the potential determinant shows a regular pattern in its values for the four types of cities. Table 4.4 has a symbol in its left-hand column for those determinants that have a regular 'gradient' from the value for the gateway cities through the stronger and moderate city types to the value for weaker cities. For example, the '+' in the same-sex couples means that the gateway cities are the type with the highest value on the measure of the proportion of such couples in the cities' populations, with the next highest value for stronger while the weaker cities have the lowest value of all the types. In the same way, the '–' in the row relating to the working-age illness variable indicates that gateway cities have the lowest value for this variable, and weaker the highest. The right-hand column

Table 4.4: Pattern of 27 non-labour-market determinants across the city types

	Regular relationship across:	
Determinant *(Change variables in italics)*	all four types	three (excluding gateway)
Demographic		
Pensionable age and over		
Under 16		
Students		
Same-sex couples	+	+
Non-EU born		–
Non-White		–
Ethnic diversification		–
Working-age illness	–	–
Standardised mortality rate	–	–
Cultural and socioeconomic		
No religion		+
High social status	+	+
Household income	+	+
Down-skilling		–
Deprivation (IMD 2000)		–
Housing market and conditions		
Turnover	+	+
Housebuilding		
Unoccupied dwellings		
Unfit dwellings		
Overcrowding		–
Owner-occupation		
Affordability	–	–
Semi-detached price	+	+
Semi-detached price increase	+	+
Environmental		
Listed buildings		+
Green space		
Burglary rate	–	–
Council Tax	–	–

Note: 'Regular relationship' denotes a progressive increase in indicator with stronger migration performance (denoted by '+') or decrease (denoted by '–'). No entry signifies that no regular relationship exists, even across the three non-gateway types. See Appendix D for the source of the variables; the variable labels here use the terms in the source data (for example, Non-White is the census term covering most minority ethnic groups). IMD 2000 = Index of Multiple Deprivation 2000.

adds some similar symbols in the rows for which these gradients only apply to the three non-gateway city types (note that it was seen in the description of labour market factors that distinctive features of the gateway cities could result in their results not necessarily being stronger than the stronger type).

Starting then with the demographic factors, the first three variables are about basic age structure and none emerges as a potential determinant on this evidence. The presence of same-sex couples is part of a relationship between economic success and more diverse and creative people that is associated with the theories of Florida in particular. By contrast, the negative values in Table 4.4 for the minority ethnic group – or non-White, to stick to census parlance – and non-EU variables undermine the support for the Florida thesis that the same-sex couples variable had offered. The other demographic variables show an expected tendency for more people to move away from less healthy cities. There are equally expected relationships with the cultural and socioeconomic variables. Cities with more people in high social status occupations – who are also more likely to have stated that they have no religion and to have higher incomes – are the cities with more positive migration balances. Equally unsurprising is that positive migration is here associated with types of cities with higher deprivation levels. The one more unfamiliar measure here reveals that the cities with more positive migration balances have seen less down-skilling (that is, a greater shift into non-manual jobs) among their workforce.

Table 4.4 also reports that there are also several housing market factors with evidence of a relationship to the relative migration balance of the four city types. Most of these housing market factors can be seen to be reflecting the well-established pattern for areas with positive migration balances to higher levels of movement in general; clearly the turnover variable fits this pattern, but arguably this is also partly driving the reason that city types with more positive migration balances tend to have high and increasing house prices along with related problems of housing affordability. A final set of factors examined in Table 4.4 is headed 'environmental' and three of the four provide evidence in support of the relationships that would have been hypothesised. The city types with more listed buildings do appear to be more attractive to migrants, as do those where there are fewer burglaries and lower Council Tax.

The role of London

The importance of London in the nation's migration patterns is a theme that has run rather consistently through our results so far. This will come as no surprise to those familiar with previous research, notably that of Coombes and Charlton (1992) and Fielding (1993). As observed above, this is directly due to the massive size of London as the UK's premier city and the distinctive composition of its migration exchanges. Moreover, to the extent that London's migration exchanges with the rest of the UK are with the other 26 cities in our sample, then the latter's migration exchanges will be affected by the nature of their relationships with the capital. It is these relationships that we probe in this section.

Exactly how important is London in the longer-distance migration exchanges of our 26 other large cities? In terms of inflows, our analyses show that the 26 cities combined saw 201,777 MGRPs moving in from the UK beyond their city regions in the year before the 2001 Census. Of these, 27,423 had been living in the London urban area 12 months earlier, or 13.6%. By contrast, London had a considerably larger pull on those leaving these cities and moving beyond their city regions, 18.7% of whom were living in the capital at the census. Moreover, the number of MGRPs involved in the outflows to London was larger than in the reverse movement, at 38,988, meaning that only seven had moved into these 26 cities from London for every 10 leaving them for the capital.

The degree of dependence on London varies greatly across the 26 cities, principally with distance from the capital – as would be expected from migration theory – but not entirely so. Figure 4.5 shows the proportion of their longer-distance migration exchanges that arrived from or departed for London, with cities ranked on the percentage of their inflows that had been living in London the year previously. That ranking is led by Brighton and

Reading, our two other gateway cities besides London and two of the five cities whose regions abut that of London (see Map 3.1). The other three that share a boundary with London – Portsmouth, Southampton and Northampton – are also quite heavily reliant on London for their inflows, although not as much as Norwich and Leicester.

Figure 4.5: Proportion of the 26 cities' MGRP exchanges with the UK beyond their city regions that are with London

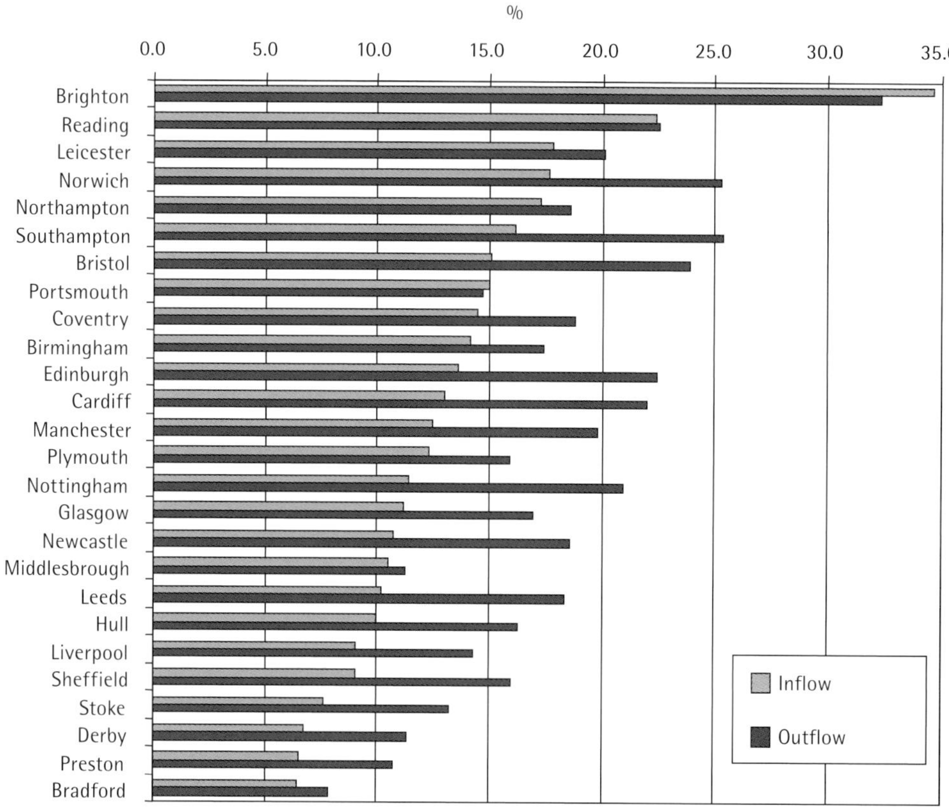

By contrast, the cities that are least dependent on London for their longer-distance inflows are largely northern cities – Bradford, Preston, Derby, Stoke, Sheffield, Liverpool and Hull (see the lower part of Figure 4.5). Other factors besides distance, however, must also play a role, given that some cities as far away from London as some of these (such as Cardiff and Manchester) and others even more distant (such as Edinburgh) appear higher up the ranking than distance alone would predict. Economic structure and role as regional/national centres would also appear to be implicated.

Turning to the degree to which the 26 cities depend on London for their longer-distance outflows, the broad picture is similar to that for inflows (as indicated by the outflow bars in Figure 4.5 generally becoming shorter as one moves down the graph). The vast majority of cities share the aggregate pattern (described above) of greater dependence on London as a destination for those leaving them than as an origin of their in-migrants. There are only two exceptions, namely Brighton and Portsmouth (just), with Reading coming next closest. By contrast, many cities have a considerable imbalance in their exchanges with London. In numerical terms, as indicated by the in/out ratio (data not shown here), the most extreme cases are Stoke, Liverpool and Hull, these receiving no more than one MGRP from London for every two leaving them for the capital.

How far do these cities' exchanges with London help to account for their prevailing weakness in relation to occupationally classified people and especially the highest skilled? The answer appears to be a great deal, according to the aggregate picture for the 26 cities presented in Table 4.5. When attention is restricted to the classified MGRPs, the in/out ratio is significantly lower than the 7:10 for all MGRPs. In the pre-census year, the 26 cities received from London only 56 MGRPs who could be classified by occupation at the census for every 100 that they lost to the capital. Looking at the four skill levels, the degree of imbalance was particularly severe for those classified as 'Higher managerial and professional' and least so for the 'Low skill' group. The ratio rises progressively with declining skill, but the outstanding result is for the 'Low skill' group: provincial cities almost 'hold their own' in their migration exchanges with London for this group, but they are losing across the board with all the higher skill groups.

Table 4.5: 26 cities' MGRP exchanges with London, classified by NS-SEC at the census

NS-SEC of MGRPs at the census	Inflows from London	Outflows to London	In/out ratio
All MGRPs	27,423	38,988	0.703
Full-time students	6,878	4,734	1.453
Other unclassified MGRPs	2,522	1,779	1.418
All occupationally classified MGRPs	18,023	32,475	0.555
Higher managerial and professional	4,447	9,339	0.476
Lower managerial and professional	6,563	13,089	0.501
Intermediate	3,279	6,129	0.535
Low	3,734	3,918	0.953

Source: Calculated from the 2001 Census SMS, Table MG109. Crown copyright

The picture becomes only marginally less depressing for the 26 cities when the aggregate of Table 4.5 is broken down into the four city types used earlier in the chapter. As shown in Figure 4.6, it is only the other two gateway cities (Brighton and Reading) that as a group managed to achieve a positive balance of classified MGRPs in their exchanges with London that year. Looking at the other cities, there is a clear relationship between overall migration strength (as represented by the three-way typology) and the level of imbalance with London, but even the stronger type appears to lose out substantially to London.

Figure 4.6: City types' migration exchanges with London, by skill level

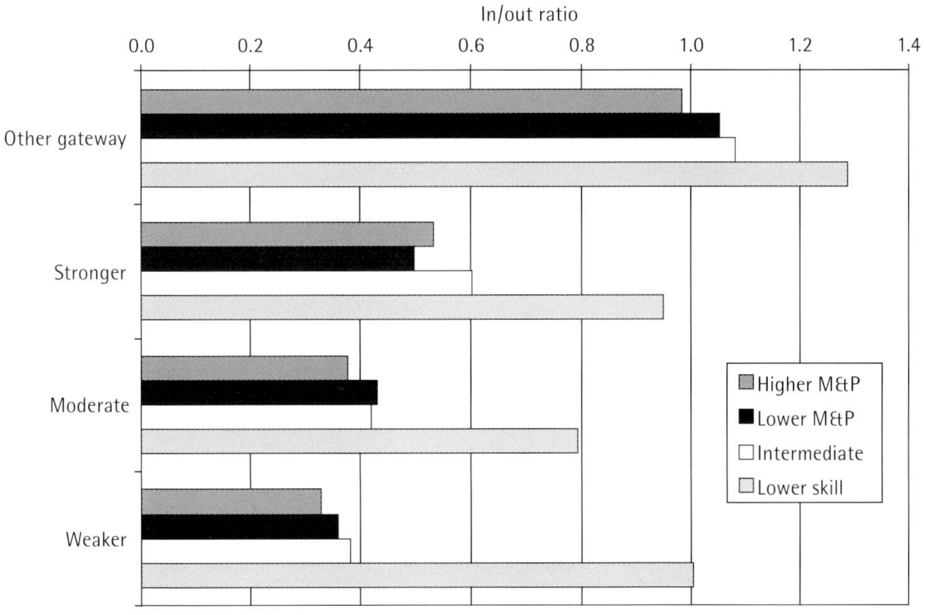

Source: Calculated from the 2001 Census SMS, Table MG109. Crown copyright

Also clear from Figure 4.6 is the important role of London in accounting for large-city Britain's greater attraction and retention of low skill people. London was seen previously (Table 4.2) as one of relatively few cities where the low skill group was not the most resilient in migration terms. Figure 4.6 shows that all four city types performed much better for this group than the other three. Indeed, Brighton and Reading combined gained five 'Low skill' MGRPs from London for every four that it lost to the capital, but both the stronger and weaker city types had a virtually even number moving in both directions and the moderate type was not far behind in this respect. By contrast, there is relatively little difference across the other three skill levels in their ratios for each city type. It would seem, therefore, that it is not just the highest skill group that London is gaining from most of the other larger cities, but the majority of the skill groups.

Breaking down this analysis to examine the 26 cities separately inevitably finds more variation and yet it also confirms both this distinctiveness of the 'Low skill' group and the similarity between the in/out ratios for the three other skill groups: with these patterns applying to almost all the cities, the explanation has to be sought in the unique role that London plays in the national pattern of human capital flows. Figure 4.7 shows the degree of variation in the cities' exchanges of 'Higher managerial and professional' MGRPs with London, with no other city coming even close to the near-balance position of the two gateway cities of Brighton and Reading. At the other end of the spectrum, Stoke received only one highly skilled MGRP from London for every six that it lost to it (note that in some cases, small numbers are involved here with, for instance, the number of 'Higher managerial and professional' MGRPs moving from Stoke to London only 106).

The results of these analyses are generally consistent with what previous studies have told us about the role of London in the UK's migration system. They show that the capital exercises a considerable hold over the migration exchanges occurring in other parts of the

Figure 4.7: 26 cities' in/out ratios for 'Higher managerial and professional' MGRP exchanges with London

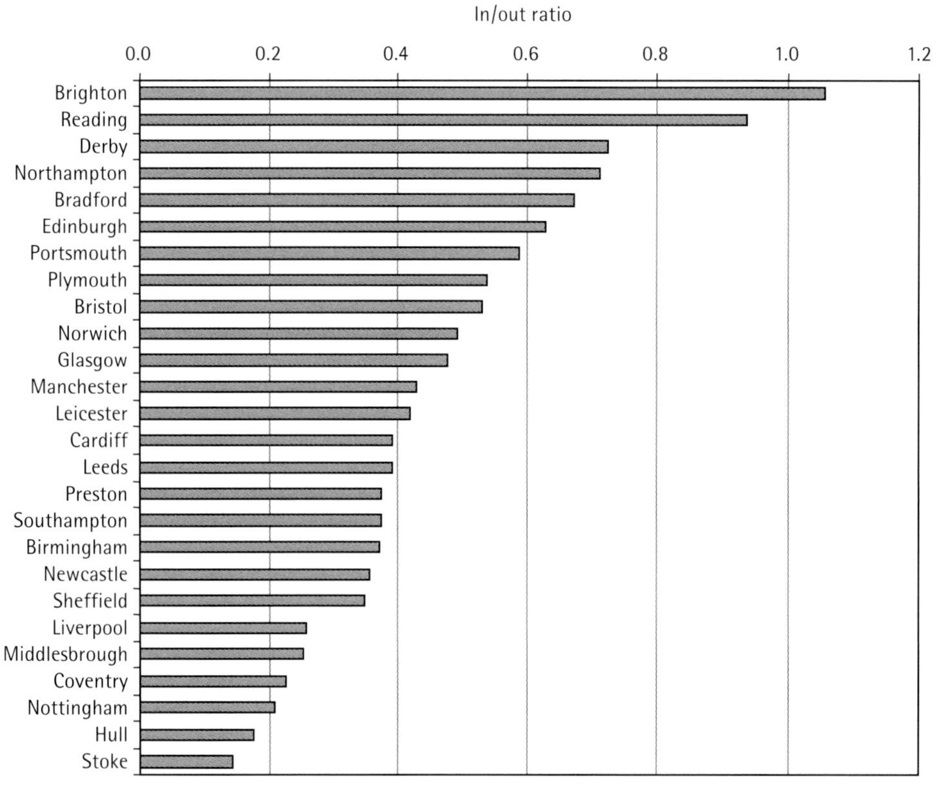

Source: Calculated from the 2001 Census SMS, Table MG109. Crown copyright

country, although the scale of this varies according to the latter's distance from London among other factors. They also demonstrate that the capital's hold is normally stronger over these other places' outflows than over their inflows. This pattern conforms to the circulatory 'life course' model of these migration flows, whereby London draws to it graduates and other young adults who are looking for the well-paid career-track jobs that are located disproportionately in this city and then sees the departure of older people who have had time to benefit from this 'hot house' environment – 'stepping off the escalator' in Fielding's (1992) terms. Moreover, what tends to happen in this process is that the aspiring youngsters are attracted from a wider area across the country than the older achievers move out to when they leave London. Indeed, to the extent that net out-migration from the London urban area begins at the age when people want a larger house for raising a family, a substantial proportion of the exodus is content to remain within London's wider city region rather than move further afield.

This well-established pattern is a hard one for other large cities to challenge, except apparently for the few that share some of London's characteristics, notably location in South East England. In fact, what we find for most cities is that the only groups that they gain from London in net terms are of people who are not in the labour market. As shown in Table 4.5, in the pre-census year the 26 cities combined received 14 of these MGRPs from London for every 10 that left them for London. This ratio was the same for 'Full-time students' as for those who at the census were 'Other unclassified' by virtue of being long-term unemployed, having never had a job or having been retired for some time. The latter will include people returning home at the end of their studies or a job contract and still seeking work. The fact that they are less common a feature of London than of most other large cities will reflect the tighter labour market in the capital and the relative dearth of suitable jobs elsewhere.

The most positive feature of most large cities, not just in their exchanges with London but in their long-distance migration more generally, is their net gain of people who were in full-time study at the time of the census. This reflects the fact that most of them contain more university places than there are families living there with members in higher education. London itself, defined on its urban areas basis (wider than just the Greater London Authority area), is unusual among cities in registering a net outflow of people going to university, but it compensates for this by having a big net gain of recent graduates. Unfortunately the census data does not allow us to investigate this further because there is no indication of which people were students one year before census day. Even so, a key issue for many provincial cities' human capital development continues to be whether they can retain more of their graduates rather than losing them to London and other parts of the country.

This brings us, finally, to consider whether the way that the census allows us to treat migration from university distorts the picture of 'human capital' movements that we have presented here. The issue is that, while we can identify people who have moved to university in the pre-census year, because they are recorded as students at the time of the census, we cannot isolate those who graduated in the pre-census year. Those recent graduates who left one of our 27 cities and got a job elsewhere in the UK, say one that involved 'Lower managerial and professional' work, before the 2001 Census will not only be recorded as an in-migrant of this type at the place they have moved to but will also be treated as a loss of this skill group for their university city. This would indeed seem to distort the picture if students moving to university were just viewed as temporary residents, as in previous censuses. Now, however, all official statistics treat moving to university as leaving the parental home, and it is increasingly being seen this way by the students themselves as they get jobs while at university, set up home and in many cases stay on there after graduation. In these circumstances, it is entirely appropriate to consider them as part of the human capital of their university cities and capable of the type of work that they get if and when they migrate somewhere else after graduation. The challenge for cities is to retain more of their graduates or, even if they lose a lot of their own graduates, to achieve a more even balance in their exchanges of such migrants with other parts of the country.

5

Population movement within the city region

We now turn to the second of the two major components of migration affecting large-city Britain, namely the shorter-distance population movement taking place between the cities and their surrounding areas. As shown in the previous chapter, these more localised flows accounted for around one quarter of the total within-UK migration exchanges of our 27 cities. Despite being numerically smaller than their longer-distance exchanges, they have the potential to make just as important an impact on the cities as the latter. This is most obviously the case in terms of the overall population change experienced by a city in a situation where its inflow was significantly different in magnitude from its outflow. It would also arise from any substantial difference in the composition of the two flows, especially where this tended to reinforce any inherited social divisions between a city's main built-up area and its wider region.

The literature tells us that both these situations are by no means uncommon for cities in Britain and elsewhere. What began as suburbanisation in the 19th century took on a much more dispersed form around cities in the 20th, culminating in the recognition of 'counter-urbanisation' in the 1970s (Champion, 2001). This latter process, involving the movement of population out of the larger cities to physically discrete settlements and more rural areas, has been observed to still be operating strongly in the UK, according to the evidence on net internal migration presented above in Figure 2.3. Moreover, just as suburbanisation predominantly involved better-off older workers in relatively secure jobs, so too the extension of this process across the wider city region is also seen as being driven largely by those of middle-age, middle-class and white ethnic background (Perry et al, 1986). The impact on cities has been conceived by some in terms of a 'stages of urban development model' that follows a downward spiral leading to the city's absolute population decline and to a widening cleavage between a more deprived urban core and a more advantaged ring of outlying areas (Hall et al, 1973).

On the other hand, this is no longer seen as an inevitable trend. Since 'gentrification' was identified in London in the 1960s, hopes have been entertained of a 'back to the city' movement that would involve not just 'bohemians' and young professionals but the general population including all stages of the life course and all strata of society. Moreover, some of the urban development models have incorporated a fully cyclic component whereby cities begin a new period of 'recentralisation', as the low land and property prices resulting from the preceding exodus encourage a new round of investment and draw residents and employers back in (Klaassen et al, 1981; Geyer and Kontuly, 1993). In Chapter 2 we noted some evidence of urban population recovery taking place in our cities in the past few years; in this chapter we turn to the question of how many of Britain's larger cities have seen an overall shift back to net migration gains from their surrounding areas, and we examine the overall social complexion of these flows to see whether they serve to reinforce or reduce social differentiation across the city region.

Migration between cities and their regions: the aggregate picture

We begin answering these questions by looking at the picture for the 27 cities combined, focusing – as in the previous chapter – on the evidence available from the census on moving groups and the classification of their reference persons (MGRPs) by occupational grouping. According to Table 5.1, the cities in aggregate appear in a much less positive light for this component of their migration than for longer-distance movement for which they made a slight net gain (as signified by the in/out ratio being above unity in Table 4.1 and now reproduced here in the final column of Table 5.1). Cities suffered a substantial overall loss through more localised movement with an in/out ratio of only 0.844 due to only 93,500 MGRPs moving into the cities from the rest of their city regions compared with nearly 111,000 moving in the opposite direction.

Table 5.1: Migration of MGRPs between cities and the rest of their city regions, by NS-SEC at the census, for 27 cities combined

NS-SEC of MGRPs at the census	Inflows	Outflows	In/out ratio	In/out ratio for longer-distance exchanges
All MGRPs	93,494	110,720	0.844	1.027
Full-time students	10,463	5,642	1.854	1.651
Other unclassified MGRPs	8,530	14,520	0.587	0.737
All occupationally classified MGRPs	74,501	90,558	0.823	0.954
Higher managerial and professional	14,043	16,284	0.862	0.998
Lower managerial and professional	25,145	30,165	0.834	0.976
Intermediate	15,714	19,447	0.808	0.930
Low	19,599	24,662	0.795	0.890

Source: Calculated from the 2001 Census SMS, Table MG109. Crown copyright

The flows are even more unbalanced for MGRPs who were not classified by occupation at the time of the census (by virtue of their being long-term unemployed, never employed, aged 75 and over, or being unclassified for any other reason besides being a student). This reflects a commonly observed sorting process whereby people who are less involved in the labour market tend to move away from the more expensive and densely populated areas close to the main centres of employment. By contrast, the migration of people who were in full-time study at the time of the census was heavily one-way into the cities from their surrounding regions, no doubt reflecting the latter's primarily residential role and the fact that many higher education institutions are located within these cities' main built-up areas.

Turning to the occupationally classified MGRPs, overall their pattern of movement in the pre-census year was again less favourable to the cities than was the case in terms of their longer-distance exchanges, with an in/out ratio of 0.823 compared with that of 0.954 for the latter. The ratio's variation across the four social groups, however, displays the same pattern as for the longer-distance movement, with the cities attracting and retaining best their highest group and with their performance declining down the social scale. The gradient across the four skill levels, however, is considerably less steep than for longer-distance migration (see Table 5.1). As such, this aggregate picture may be even more sensitive to the effect of one or two of the largest cities than was found in Chapter 4.

Migration between cities and their regions: the 27 cities individually

How representative of all the 27 cities is this aggregate picture of rather low overall in/out ratio, alongside a positive relationship between city attraction/retention and social status? As found in previous analyses, it is again the case that London is rather distinctive and, because of its massive size, it is tending to dominate the totals. As shown in Figure 5.1, London's in/out ratio for all MGRPs is among the lowest of the 27 cities. It is on a par only with the country's second largest city (Birmingham), a couple of other cities that performed weakly in relation to longer-distance migration (Bradford and Coventry) and one of the other two cities that we have classified as gateway (Brighton). A few cities saw substantially more MGRPs moving in from the rest of their regions than in the opposite direction, notably Plymouth, Norwich, Portsmouth and Southampton, but the majority picture is of overall deconcentration from city to their surroundings, although to a lesser degree than London experienced.

Moreover, given the centripetal movement of students noted in Table 5.1, it is not surprising to find that the pattern for occupationally classified MGRPs is even less positive for the 27 cities. As shown in Table 5.2 (first data column), just seven cities recorded a higher inflow than outflow of these in their exchanges with the rest of their regions.

Figure 5.1: In/out ratio for 27 cities' migration exchanges with the rest of their city regions: all MGRPs

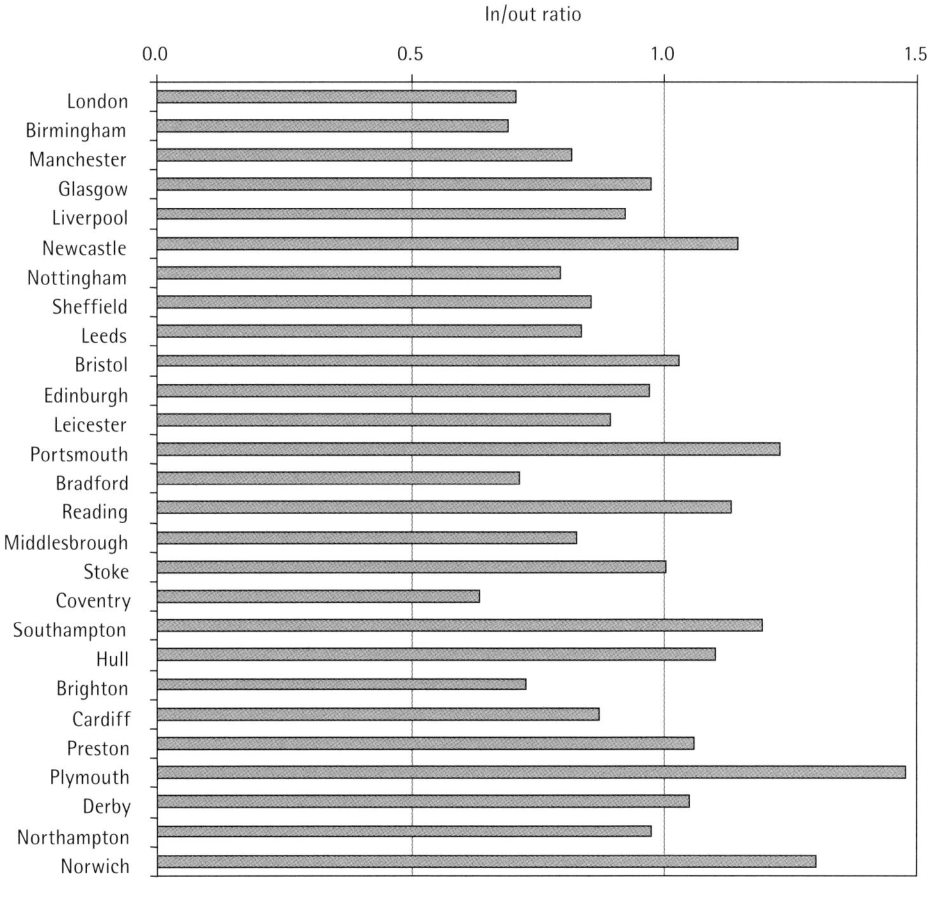

Source: Calculated from the 2001 Census SMS, Table MG109. Crown copyright

This proportion of only around a quarter of cities with an in/out ratio above unity is also found for those classified as 'Higher managerial and professional' at the census (Table 5.2, second data column), and the same is true of the other three social groups (data not shown). Moreover, the list of these cities is relatively stable across the social scale, with Plymouth, Norwich and Portsmouth registering above-unity ratios for all four social groups and Southampton, Reading and Bristol doing so for three of the four groups. By contrast, over half of the 27 cities saw more moving out than moving in for all four social groups, and London was one of these, putting it into a very different situation compared with its position in relation to longer-distance migration.

Table 5.2: In/out ratio for 27 cities' migration exchanges with the rest of their city regions: all classified, 'Higher managerial and professional', and four skill groups ranked

City (arranged by size)	In/out ratio for all classified MGRPs	In/out ratio for Higher M&P MGRPs	Ranking of skill group on in/out ratio (1 = highest)			
			Higher M&P	Lower M&P	Inter-mediate	Low skill
London	0.720	0.884	1	2	3	4
Birmingham	0.671	0.546	4	3	2	1
Manchester	0.806	0.816	2	3	1	4
Glasgow	0.895	1.138	1	3	2	4
Liverpool	0.923	0.937	2	1	4	3
Newcastle	1.042	0.962	4	3	1	2
Nottingham	0.812	0.642	4	3	2	1
Sheffield	0.820	0.788	3	4	2	1
Leeds	0.742	0.790	2	3	1	4
Bristol	1.027	1.074	2	3	1	4
Edinburgh	0.815	0.754	4	2	1	3
Leicester	0.846	0.604	4	3	1	2
Portsmouth	1.106	1.079	2	1	3	4
Bradford	0.740	0.750	2	3	4	1
Reading	1.126	1.235	1	3	2	4
Middlesbrough	0.744	0.604	4	1	2	3
Stoke	0.993	0.612	4	3	2	1
Coventry	0.814	0.553	4	3	1	2
Southampton	1.157	0.956	4	3	2	1
Hull	0.844	0.492	4	3	2	1
Brighton	0.720	0.739	1	2	4	3
Cardiff	0.791	0.891	1	3	2	4
Preston	0.964	0.934	3	2	4	1
Plymouth	1.372	1.235	3	4	2	1
Derby	0.987	0.705	3	4	1	2
Northampton	0.948	1.038	1	4	2	3
Norwich	1.255	1.243	3	2	4	1

Source: Calculated from the 2001 Census SMS, Table MG109. Crown copyright

In one respect, however, London's performance on this more localised migration is similar to that for its longer-distance exchanges. As shown in Table 5.2 (last four columns), London displays a clear positive relationship between in/out ratio and social status, such that the ratio is highest for the highest social group and declines progressively down the social scale (just as found for the capital's longer-distance migration in Table 4.2 above).

Unlike the impression conveyed in the aggregate picture of Table 5.1, this is by no means the majority experience among the 27 cities. Indeed, in Table 5.2 there is no other city besides London that has exactly that '1-2-3-4' grading of ratios by social group, only one other city – Brighton – that has the same '12' element of this, and only four further cities where the 'Higher managerial and professional' group had the highest ratio (signified by '1' in the first column), these being Reading, Northampton, Cardiff and Glasgow. By contrast, the 'Higher managerial and professional' group scored the lowest in/out ratio for as many as 10 cities and, moreover, there was a regular negative relationship (signified by '4-3-2-1') across the social groups for fully half these (Birmingham, Nottingham, Stoke, Southampton and Hull).

Relationship with longer-distance migration

To what extent do the cities' experiences in relation to their migration exchanges with their city regions parallel those observed for their longer-distance migration, so that the two processes tend to reinforce each other in their effects? Rather than trying to compare all the detail of Table 5.2 with that of the equivalent analysis for longer-distance migration (Table 4.2), we present more summary information in Figure 5.2 based on the four city types used in Chapter 4. Those types are based on the 27 cities' performance in relation to longer-distance migration (including international migration in the case of the gateway cities). Thus, any conformity with the patterns for longer-distance migration shown in Figure 4.3 will indicate that the more localised migration exchanges are reinforcing the latter, whereas divergence from that pattern would be indicative of a reciprocal or offsetting relationship.

Comparing the patterns in Figure 5.2 with those in Figure 4.3 suggests one clear difference between the more localised and the longer-distance migration exchanges. This relates to the overall picture of migration for the gateway cities. Whereas this type of city was the strongest performing of the four types in its longer-distance migration exchanges, it turns

Figure 5.2: City types' in/out ratios with the rest of their city regions

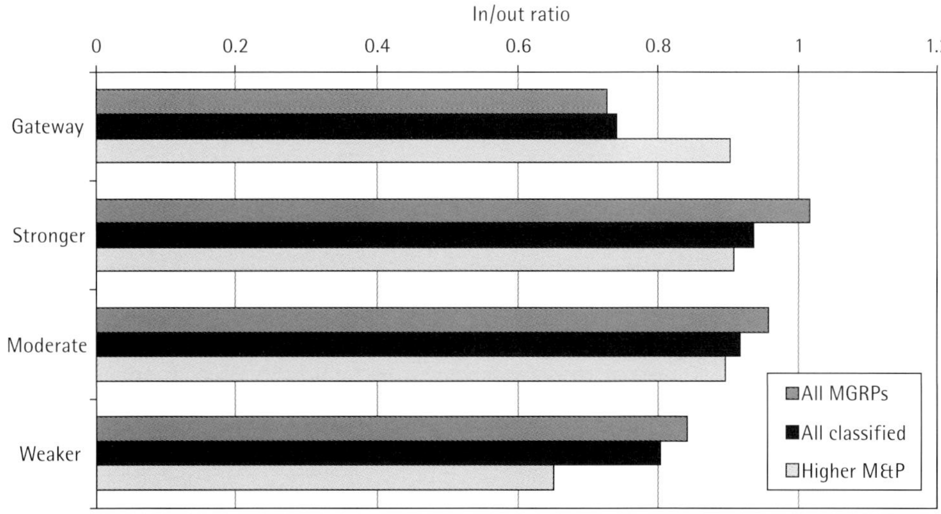

Source: Calculated from the 2001 Census SMS, Table MG109. Crown copyright

out to be the weakest in terms of its city/city region exchanges for all the categories of MRGPs except the most highly skilled group.

This is in contrast to the very clear parallels between the shorter and longer-distance components of migration across the other three city types revealed by comparing Figures 5.2 and 4.3. Certainly, in relation to all MGRPs and the aggregate of the occupationally classified ones, the cities that fared the best in their exchanges with the UK beyond their city region boundaries were also the ones that, at least when grouped together like this, registered the most positive balances with their city regions. Similarly, the cities defined as 'weaker' in their longer-distance exchanges were also the type that performed most weakly of the three non-gateway types in terms of their more local migration.

There are also clear parallels between the two components in the patterning of the three migration measures for each type of city (cf Figures 5.2 and 4.3). For both longer-distance and more local migration, the in/out ratios for the gateway type are higher for all classified MGRPs than for all MGRPs, and are more positive again for the 'Higher managerial and professional' group. This demonstrates that the gateway type is better at attracting and retaining the highest social group than other people, irrespective of migration distance. For the three other city types, the reverse is the case, with all of them performing more weakly in both types of migration when students and other unclassified MGRPs are taken out of the equation, and even worse when just the highest social group is being considered.

Finally, just focusing on this 'Higher managerial and professional' group, the picture conveyed by Figure 5.2 is that there is not much relationship between city performance on longer-distance migration (which forms the basis of the city types) and performance on the more local exchanges. The only clear feature is the much lower in/out ratios for the weaker group, with those for the three other groups being very evenly matched. In fact, however, if the two components of 'Higher managerial and professional' migration are plotted against each other for the 27 cities individually, as in Figure 5.3, a positive association is found between the two. In general, the better that cities fared in their exchanges with the rest of the UK on this high skill group in the pre-census year, the better they also fared in terms of this group's migration with the rest of their city regions.

On the basis of this evidence, then, the gateway type of city is indeed rather distinct from the other cities. This type is relatively attractive to longer-distance migration – including international migration, as this was the criterion on which its three members were isolated from the other 24 cities – but loses out to the surrounding region. The two types of migration thus operate in a reciprocal relationship, with the gains from longer-distance migration being offset by losses more locally. This pattern is indicative of a dynamic situation where the local exodus acts as a type of safety valve that keeps the lid on the build-up of pressures at the core of the city region. This situation is also reflected in the socioeconomic complexion of the population movements, with those in 'Higher managerial and professional' work being keener and/or better able to access the city than people in general. Of course, this interpretation benefits from knowing that London drives this city type, but in fact Brighton shares the capital's pattern of gain from longer-distance migration and loss to its local region while Reading is equally attractive to the 'Higher managerial and professional' group for both distances of migration.

At the other end of the spectrum is the weaker city type. While it displays a level of migrant loss to the rest of the city region similar to that of the gateway type, there is – for the group as a whole anyway – no compensating migration gain from the rest of the UK nor, by definition, from overseas. Both longer-distance and more local migration exchanges are eating into the stock of human capital represented by the residents of this city type. Moreover, this process is one in which 'Higher managerial and professional' people are more heavily involved than are other types of people. As a 'double whammy', this looks

Figure 5.3: The 27 cities' in/out ratios of exchanges of 'Higher managerial and professional' MGRPs with the rest of UK plotted against those with the rest of their city regions

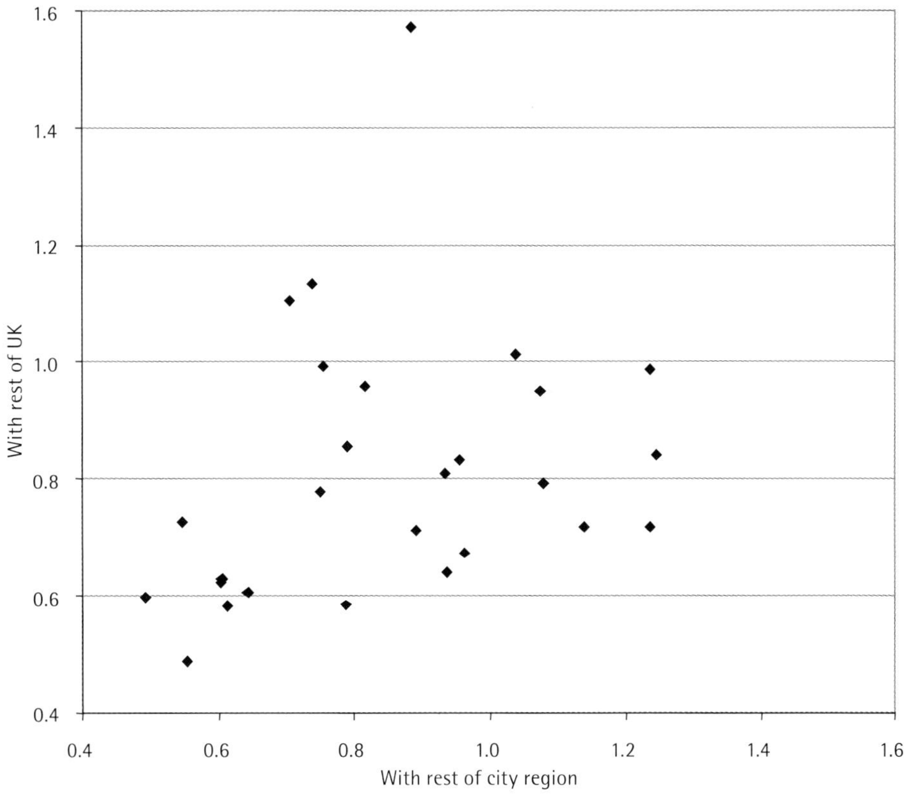

Source: Calculated from the 2001 Census SMS, Table MG109. Crown copyright

like a situation that can lead to a decline in both the size and the quality of a city's labour force, most obviously through losing population to beyond the city region boundary but also through the more local exodus to the extent that out-migrants to the outer part of the city's region may end up working closer to their new home rather than continuing to work in the main urban area. Certainly, the combined processes could lead to a weakening of the city's housing market, a reduction in investor confidence and possibly a downward spiral where losses from one type of migration make the city generally less attractive for its people to live and work in.

Finally, turning to what we have called the stronger and moderate city types, these both perform more robustly than the gateway and weaker ones in terms of their exchanges with their city regions of both all MGRPs and all classified MGRPs. Nevertheless, in terms of the latter, these two groups are losing out both to their surrounding regions and further afield, but just not as severely as the weaker type. The evidence suggests that the same applies even more forcefully to their exchanges of the highest social group than to the other occupational levels, although the margin of difference from the all-classified average is small for both types and both distances of migration.

Factors underlying migration between cities and their regions

According to the analyses above, across our 27 cities there is a prevailing situation of population deconcentration, whereby more MGRPs are moving out of the main built-up area to the rest of the city region than are moving in the opposite direction. Clearly, the signs of urban population recovery noted in Chapter 2 have not yet involved a complete reversal of this well-established process. This situation is easier to understand in the cases of the gateway and stronger city types, given that these are gaining from longer-distance migration and tend to have limits imposed on land release for new housing. Such deconcentration seems much less justified, and indeed much less desirable for cities that have a negative migration balance with the rest of the UK. This section aims to discover what lies behind the movements taking place within the city region in the pre-census year, by examining how the place characteristics generally recognised to act as 'push' and 'pull' factors in migration differ between the cities and their regions across the four city types. This provides the context within which, in the final section, we analyse more localised patterns of movement within three city regions drawn from the gateway, stronger and weaker types.

In examining the sorts of factors that might underlie the prevailing centrifugal trend of within-region migration indicated by Figure 5.2, we adopt a similar approach to that used to explore the factors underlying variations between city types in their longer-distance migration (see Figure 4.4 and Table 4.4). Table 5.3 lists the full set of migration determinants analysed there and, in the left hand column, compares the scores for the cities with those of their wider city regions. An 'H' indicates that, across all four city types, the score for the city is higher than the score for the city region, while an 'L' indicates that it is lower for all four city types. Where there is no entry, this indicates that there is no systematic pattern across the four city types.

The entries in the first column of Table 5.3 enable us to identify what characteristics of cities might predispose them to losing out in their shorter-distance migration exchanges, especially those involving the 'Higher managerial and professional' group. In terms of demographic characteristics, the cities contain a smaller proportion of people of pensionable age than their wider city regions but the larger proportions of students, same-sex couples, people born outside the EU and non-Whites. Compared with their city regions, the cities also saw faster growth in their proportions of non-Whites between 1991 and 2001, and had higher levels of long-term limiting illness among their working-age people.

There are also a number of consistent differences (at least at the level of the four city types) among the other sets of determinants listed in Table 5.3. Compared with their surrounding regions, the cities are characterised by higher levels of deprivation, population turnover, unfit dwellings, overcrowding (persons per room) and burglary. They also have higher levels of down-skilling (that is, a slower or negative shift out of manual work during 1991-2001), employment, educational attainment, local job growth, longer-distance commuting by residents, housebuilding, owner-occupation, affordability, listed buildings and green space (proportion of land not built-up).

Most of these patterns are quite easy to interpret in relation to the prevailing urban exodus, as they are in line with prior expectations (see, for instance, the analysis of urban exodus by Champion et al, 1998b). It is expected that people will try to avoid living in areas of deprivation, poorer school results, overcrowding, higher housing costs and lower healthiness and seek out areas with more housebuilding, more owner-occupied properties, stronger job growth and more green space. Moreover, 'Higher managerial and professional' people are likely to be keener than most to distance themselves from what are generally seen as 'push' factors and will certainly be in a better financial position than others to achieve this.

Some other patterns, however, do not lend themselves quite so readily to a clear explanation. The stronger representation of students, same-sex couples and people of immigrant stock is viewed normally (as in Chapter 4) as a sign of the strength and attractiveness of cities, so this could be associated with the build-up of population pressures that might prompt an 'overspill' to the surrounding region, as discussed above

Table 5.3: Migration determinants for four city types: ratio of cities to their city regions

Determinant (change variables in italics)	City generally higher (H) or lower (L) than city region	Stronger city type higher (H) or lower (L) than weaker
Demographic		
Pensionable age and over	L	L
Under 16		
Students	H	H
Same-sex couples	H	H
Non-EU born	H	L
Non-White	H	L
Ethnic diversification	H	L
Working-age illness	H	
Standardised mortality rate		
Cultural and socioeconomic		
No religion		H
High social status		H
Household income		H
Down-skilling	H	H
Deprivation (IMD 2000)	H	L
Labour market		
Employment rate	L	H
Employment rate change	L	H
School leavers with 5(+) GCSEs	L	
Graduate workforce		H
Local job growth	L	H
Commuting 10km(+)	L	H
Housing market and conditions		
Turnover	H	H
Housebuilding	L	
Unoccupied dwellings		L
Unfit dwellings	H	L
Overcrowding	H	L
Owner-occupation	L	
Affordability	L	
Semi-detached price		H
Semi-detached price increase		H
Environmental		
Listed buildings	L	H
Green space	L	
Burglary rate	H	
Council Tax		

Note: Blank denotes not clearly higher or lower across all four city types (left-hand column) and little difference between stronger and weaker (right-hand column). See Appendix D for the full specification and source of the characteristics.

in relation to gateway and stronger cities. For weaker cities, however, this would seem unlikely, so there might be some element of 'flight' involved here. Yet other patterns are as likely to be consequences as causes of the prevailing trend, such as the higher proportion of older people in the wider city region, or features that are already associated with the more outlying parts of a city region, such as longer-distance commuting.

Moving on to the right-hand column of Table 5.3, this attempts to explain the differential performance of the cities with respect to their level of population loss to their regions. It does this by comparing the stronger with the weaker city type on the degree to which the city's value exceeds that of the city region, with 'H' indicating greater for the stronger type, 'L' denoting greater for the weaker type and a blank indicating no marked difference between the two. In terms of demography, for instance, the stronger city type has a higher differential over its surrounding region for the presence of students and same-sex couples in their population than does the weaker type, but it is the weaker cities – characterised by their higher out-migration – that have the higher ratio over their city regions for older people and in relation to ethnic diversity.

Again, some of the patterns shown in this column are easier to interpret than others. Some may be more an effect of the migration process than a cause; for example, the greater similarity in the elderly shares of city and region for the weaker cities that may well reflect the faster ageing of the city brought about by the greater exodus of young people. The weaker type's larger city/region differential for the non-EU born and non-Whites, too, may have arisen through selective migration, as well as possibly through the greater pressures in the stronger type prompting a greater local decentralisation of these population groups. The stronger type's higher city/region differential in house prices is also likely to be a reflection of their greater power to retain population within their main built-up area. Perhaps this is also the case in relation to the stronger cities having more high-status people and higher average household incomes than their surrounding regions (unlike the weaker cities where the reverse applies), although equally this could help these cities retain and attract residents.

Some other characteristics, however, are more likely to be drivers of the poorer performances of the weaker cities in relation to their city/region migration exchanges. In particular, labour market considerations, although not expected to loom as large in within-region moves as in longer-distance migration, appear to contribute to the success of the stronger cities in bucking the centrifugal tendency. The much less buoyant situation of the weaker cities compared with their regions in this respect will be a major disincentive to move into the city from the surrounding region and an equal incentive for the city's residents to move out to where job growth is proceeding rapidly. In addition, employers may well be more tempted to invest in the more outlying areas with their greater presence of graduates, even if the workers living in these areas tend to have a higher propensity to commute longer distances relative to those in their cities than is the case for the stronger cities.

Migration within three city regions

What we have done so far in this chapter on population movement within the city region is to look at people moving between the city and the rest of the city region and relate these flows to the way in which these two parts of the city region differ from each other. By itself, however, this provides only a partial understanding of the dynamics of residential movement across the city region. For one thing, the changes of address that take place across the edge of the city's main built-up area comprise only a small proportion of the total movement taking place, even if one excludes the most localised moves (say, those of under 5km) from the equation. For another, neither part of the city region is a homogeneous entity but will be characterised by a certain amount of internal differentiation, not least in terms of social patterning. Moreover, when people are thinking about moving house, they can be expected to be quite sensitive to these sorts of differences between the smaller localities that make up each of these two parts of the city region. Indeed, they may well be much more influenced by these more local features than whether they are living on one side or the other of the main built-up area's boundary, even though the latter may be clearly demarcated on the map as a result of greenbelt designation and other building restrictions.

Part of our study, therefore, has involved analysing patterns of migration for a more detailed geography of the city region than just the two-way split between the main built-up area of the city and the rest of its city region. Resources permitted an exploratory study using three city regions. The rationale for the selection of our case studies is spelt out in Appendix E, along with details of how we divided these city regions up into smaller localities. In brief, our three city regions include one example each from three of the four city types used in the 27-city analysis: London as a gateway city, Bristol as a stronger city and Birmingham as a weaker city. As regards their subdivision into localities, we were more concerned about having a reasonably consistent number in each city region than about them being a consistent population size across the three city regions (which, given that London is eight times more populous than Bristol, would have led to very different numbers between city regions). Partly due to considerations of data availability, we limited ourselves to using local authority districts and 'tracts' (Dorling et al, 2004) as building blocks for the localities, ending up with 46 for London's city region, 34 for Bristol's and 60 for Birmingham's.

A central interest in this part of the study was the extent to which the within-region migration behaviour that we observe from the 2001 Census has served to reinforce existing patterns of social differentiation between the city region's localities of each city region or to reduce them. To answer this question, we calculated the in/out ratios for the exchanges between each locality and the rest of the city region for each of our four occupationally classified groups, and then compared these with the existing importance of the relevant group in each locality. As an example, Figure 5.4 shows the result of plotting the in/out ratios of 'Higher managerial and professional' MGRPs against this group's share of all classified residents for each of the 46 localities of London's city region. In this case, no clear relationship is evident, confirmed by a correlation coefficient (r) of just +0.006 (using a logged version of the in/out ratio). On that basis, it is concluded that the within-region migration in the pre-census year was neither reinforcing nor reducing the degree of between-locality differentiation in this respect.

The correlation results for all four social groups for all three city regions are presented in Table 5.4. Unlike that for the 'Higher managerial and professional' group in London's city region, those for the other three social groups there are all highly significant. The patterning of the migration, however, differs between them. In the case of the 'Lower managerial and professional' group, the coefficient indicates that there is an inverse relationship between the in/out ratio and the existing level of representation of this group. The more important this group already was in a locality, the lower its revealed attractiveness for in-migrants of this type relative to the numbers moving away to somewhere else in the city region. The effect of this one year's worth of movement by MGRPs classified in this group at the census was thus to reduce the unevenness of this group's distribution across the city region. For the two lowest social groups, by contrast, the strong positive coefficients indicate that this year's migration flows served to reinforce the inherited differentials.

The results for Birmingham's city region are quite different from this. Here it is the movement of the two highest social groups that are reinforcing the between-locality

Figure 5.4: Inflow/outflow ratio of within-region exchanges of 'Higher managerial and professional' MGRPs plotted against this group's share of classified residents, for the 46 localities of London's city region

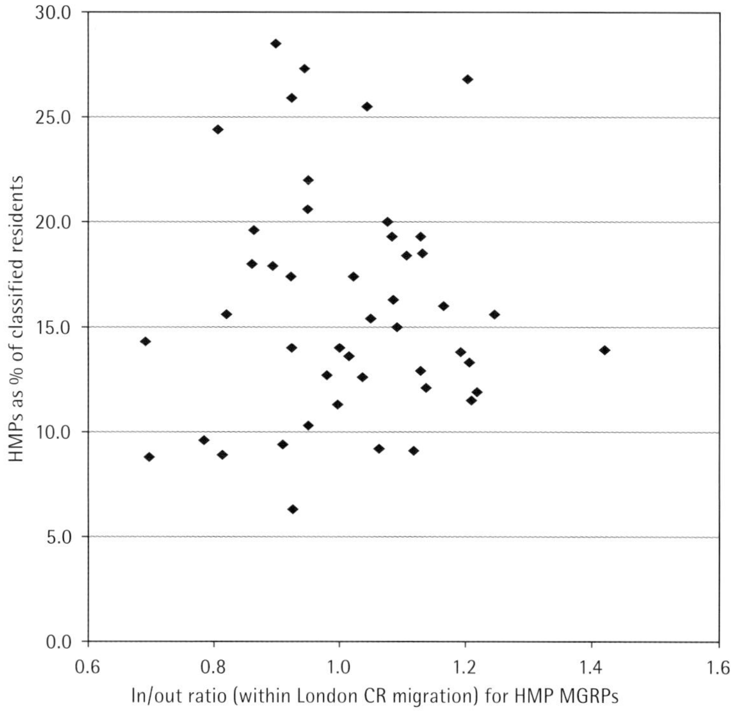

Source: Calculated from the 2001 Census SMS, Table MG109, and 2001 Census commissioned table. Crown copyright

variations in the inherited patterning of these groups, while there is no social group that migrated in such a way as to noticeably reduce local levels of social segregation. In the case of Bristol's city region, the coefficients are positive for all four social groups, suggesting an overall tendency towards this migration reinforcing the existing social patterns, but the relationships are all weak, not even reaching the 5% significance level (although quite close to it for the 'Low skill' group).

The overall picture conveyed by the results for the three case study regions, therefore, is of this within-region migration generally being in conformity with the existing social differentials between localities, but this is generally a rather weak process, with considerable departure from a 'perfect' relationship. Viewed from a somewhat different perspective, even the highly significant coefficients found for London's 'Intermediate' and 'Low skill' groups represent a 'level of explanation' (R^2) of under one third (32 and 29% respectively). In the case of Birmingham, the existing social patterning accounts for less than 10% of the between-locality variance in in/out ratios for the two managerial and professional groups.

Indeed, it might perhaps be considered surprising that these associations are not more positive. It might be expected that this migration would have contributed to the configurations of socioeconomic differentiation observed from the 2001 Census. While one year's worth of migration by itself is hardly likely to have had a big impact, past research and migration theory suggest that migration streams have a long-term momentum, normally remaining rather stable over many years (as reflected in the little change observed by Champion and Fisher, 2003, in the largest conurbations' migration between 1981 and 1991). On the other hand, this is not the only process leading to social change in the population, nor necessarily the most important. As mentioned at the start of the chapter, the migration exchanges with the rest of the UK and international migration will be operating alongside the within-region movement and also helping to alter the social

Table 5.4: Correlations (r) between in/out ratios of four social groups and proportions of classified residents in the relevant social group, for the localities of three city regions

NS-SEC grouping of classified MGRPs	London (*n*=46)	Birmingham (*n* =60)	Bristol (*n* =34)
Higher managerial and professional	+0.006	+0.314	+0.045
Lower managerial and professional	-0.466	+0.304	+0.037
Intermediate	+0.566	-0.012	+0.043
Low	+0.538	+0.081	+0.268

Note: n = number of localities. Logged versions of the in/out ratios have been used. For London, coefficients of 0.377 and above are significant at the 1% level, those of 0.291 and above at the 5% level. The equivalent thresholds for Birmingham are 0.329 and 0.255 respectively, for Bristol 0.438 and 0.341.

Source: Calculated from the 2001 Census SMS, Table MG109, and 2001 Census commissioned table. Crown copyright

complexion of the city regions, let alone the indigenous social restructuring taking place in the non-migrant residents who form the majority of these areas' populations.

Conversely, however, the geographical concentrations of particular social groups that have evolved via all these longer-term processes of residential sorting and community development do not seem to be exercising a dominant influence on this one year of within-region migration. One possible explanation for the dissonance between the two is that migration behaviour is, in fact, undergoing a phase of change, whereby the more recent migrants are no longer seeking out the destinations that their predecessors selected. This is what one might expect if the capacity of a locality to receive further in-migrants was reaching its limits, with the resultant house price inflation forcing potential incomers of a particular income group to search elsewhere for affordable accommodation. This can occur on a relatively short-term basis during the course of an economic cycle, as has been documented in terms of the relationships between migration patterns and the 'house price ripple' (Brunsdon et al, 1991). Certainly, the pre-census year 2000-01 occurred at just about the time when the ripple in the latest house price cycle was moving rapidly out from London across England and could well have been distorting migration away from its 'average' pattern then.

Whether or not there was some long-term or cyclical switch in migration patterns just before the 2001 Census, it is also the case that migration decisions take into account a variety of factors, with people wanting to live close to 'people like us' (Hickman et al, 2007) being only one consideration among many. With this in mind, we examined the correlation between in/out ratios and over 40 variables representing characteristics that were considered to possibly affect the attractiveness of localities for residents and in-migrants (see Appendix D for the full list). Then we used multiple regression analysis to model the migration patterns and identify the main characteristics that each play their separate roles in driving and fashioning them. For reasons of space, we present the results just for one social group, selecting the 'Higher managerial and professional' one because of its central interest for our study and also because it is this group that has the greatest choice of home location. To limit further the detail presented here, the correlation analyses are reported in Appendix F: these analyses lead to the development of a reduced set of 15 variables for regression analyses and it is their results that follow here.

Table 5.5 shows the results of the regression analysis on the in/out ratios of the 'Higher managerial and professional' group at the locality scale. Results are shown for the three city regions side by side. The model for London is the most successful of the three in terms of the proportion of the variance in the in/out ratios of this group across the region's 46 localities that it manages to account for (69%). It is also the most complex. In all, 11 of the

Table 5.5: Results of regression analyses performed on localities' in/out ratios of the within-region migration of 'Higher managerial and professional' MGRPs for three city regions

Locality characteristics *(change variables in italics)*	London (*n*=46)	Birmingham (*n*=60)	Bristol (*n*=34)
Demographic			
Under 16	+		
Students	–		–
Cultural and socioeconomic			
No religion	+		
Ethnic diversification	+		
Down-skilling	–	–	
Household income	+		+
Labour market			
Employment rate	–	+	
Employment rate change	+		
Local job growth	–		+
Commuting 10km(+)			
Housing			
Semi-detached price			
Semi-detached price change		+	+
Unoccupied dwellings	+		
Environmental			
Green space	+		
Crime			+
Adjusted R2	0.693	0.301	0.398

Note: The dependent variable is the in/out ratio logged. The models have been derived by backward regression. Only those variables significant at the 5% level have been retained in the final models. See Appendix F for the full specification and source of the characteristics.
Source: The dependent variable is calculated from the 2001 Census SMS, Table MG109. Crown copyright

15 variables offered to the model have been identified as separately contributing to the migration patterns of this group.

Looking at the specific characteristics in the London model, demographics provides two separate drivers for 'Higher managerial and professional' MGRPs, with this group appearing to seek out localities where school-age children are more prevalent and also shunning those with high concentrations of students. All four cultural and socioeconomic factors are seen as playing a contributory role, as shown by the positive associations with average household income, the proportion of people with no religious affiliation, the lack of down-skilling in the workforce and the rate at which the proportion of non-White people is increasing. There is a positive role for the rate at which the proportion of working-age people in employment is rising, but the level of the employment rate and the rate of job growth in and around the locality appears to work as a deterrent for this group. Finally, again allowing for all the other variables included in the model, there are also separate roles for the proportion of unoccupied dwellings and the share of total land area not yet built over, such that the more there is of these two, the greater is the attractive power of the locality for this group.

By contrast, the model derived from the data for the 60 localities of Birmingham's city region is much less successful in accounting for the variance in in/out ratios across its 60 localities (just 30%). It is also much simpler in structure, with just three of the 15 variables included. The localities most attractive to 'Higher managerial and professional' MGRPs there were those with the highest levels of working-age people in employment, the lowest rate of down-skilling and, in addition, the fastest rise in house prices. Note that, in this type of analysis, these three are all playing a separate role in statistical terms, accounting for a different element of the variance. This evidence (taken in conjunction with the information in Table A6.2) suggests that this group is clearly ending up in 'commuter' localities and especially places that are already high status and/or are moving strongly in that direction. Interestingly, this picture has only one element in common with the model for London: the low level of down-skilling over the previous decade.

Finally, the model for Bristol's city region lies in between the other two in more ways than one. It is moderately successful, accounting for 40% of the variance in this high skill group's in/out ratios across the region's 34 localities – this despite having only one significant variable in simple correlation. Five of the 15 characteristics offered to the model contribute towards this explanation. 'Higher managerial and professional' MGRPs are least attracted to the parts of the city region with the most students and gravitate most to localities with the highest household incomes as well as to those with the strongest local job growth, those with fastest increases in house prices and those with the greatest crime. The latter goes against conventional wisdom, suggesting that there is an element of this high skill movement that is moving into certain areas despite their higher crime rates, these probably being inner-city areas favoured by recent graduates (given that some of the highest positive correlations with crime in this city region are with students, people with no religious affiliation, rented accommodation and increase in the non-White share of the population). As such, the overall model bears certain affinities with both London's (shunning students and seeking out high income areas) and Birmingham's (associated with high house price inflation).

The message from these analyses seems to be two-fold. In the first place, a good deal of the within-region movement of the 'Higher managerial and professional' group tends to conform to expectation, being attracted to high status or upwardly mobile areas, localities with more open space and so on. At the same time, the fact that several 'drivers' are identified as contributing separately to the observed patterns in each model (although arguably only one major one in Birmingham's case) suggests a certain degree of multidimensionality to the phenomenon. This latter conclusion is reinforced by the rather high level of variance still unaccounted for, especially in the Birmingham and Bristol cases. This is not surprising, given that our target group is a broad one, not only grouping together several of the original NS-SEC categories but also spanning the full age range 16-74 and combining people from different ethnic origins, household types, housing situations and so on. Allowing for the effect of all these influences would call for analyses of data on individual people, but there is no available micro-level data both with sufficient records and with sufficiently localised coding of the former and current addresses of migrants.

6

Conclusions and implications

As part of the Joseph Rowntree Foundation's Census Research Programme, this study has explored what the 2001 Census can tell us about how Britain's larger cities are faring in their migration exchanges with each other and the rest of the UK. In particular, recognising that for many policy-related purposes the 'quality of human capital' characteristics of this migration are just as important as the sheer numbers involved, our work has focused on the occupational level and social status of cities' inflows and outflows, giving most attention to the 'Higher managerial and professional' group. In this context, we have taken full advantage of several innovations in the migration data provided as standard output from the latest census that have not been available from previous enumerations, especially the inclusion of counts of migration by socioeconomic classification in the origin destination statistics and the treatment of movement to and from university as change of usual address. Appendix G assesses how far the census, by itself, can take us in answering the types of questions that researchers are asking in this area of study, and how far other forms of analysis are also needed. That said, it is essential to reiterate that without the census it would not be possible for analyses of the sort reported here to be attempted. Only a census can provide the necessary size of sample, with its detailed variable coding and locational referencing.

The purposes of this final chapter are to summarise our principal findings and to discuss their policy significance so far as this can be confidently assessed.

Principal findings

Large-city Britain is still losing population through migration flows with the rest of the UK

It is important to make this point: the 2001 Census data – in indicating that in the pre-census year the 27 cities examined in this study lost over 60,000 people through their migration with the rest of the UK – confirms the overall picture provided by other sources, notably the continuous monitoring of internal migration based on NHS records. In fact, those other sources indicate no long-term diminution in the scale of the urban exodus, instead revealing a rising trajectory since the beginning of the 1990s. The urban population recovery observed in recent years has its origins elsewhere, notably in international migration trends. This in no way undermines the continuing importance of achieving a better understanding of within-UK population movement and how it may be changing in geographical pattern, social composition and driving forces.

The majority of large cities display weaker migration balances for higher skill people

More than half of the study's 27 cities, as defined on a built-up area basis rather than just their administrative district, displayed weaker performances on their within-UK migration balances for the 'Higher managerial and professional' group than for all occupationally classified movers, as measured by the ratio of in-migrants to out-migrants. In fact, on the basis of the four occupational groups used for this study, the prevailing picture was one of a negative association between skill level and in/out ratio, with most cities doing best at retaining and/or attracting the 'Low skill' group. On the other hand, people moving to attend university represent a major source of population growth for cities, although data on the net movement of 20- to 24-year-olds suggests that many cities have difficulty in retaining their own universities' graduates and/or attracting those from elsewhere.

Cities' performance on long-distance migration is similar to that on more local exchanges

When the cities were classified on the strength of their in/out ratios for migration with the rest of the UK beyond their city region boundaries – which makes up around three quarters of their total inflows and outflows – the pattern found was similar to that with respect to the remainder of their own city regions. In particular, the weaker cities type was seen to suffer the 'double whammy' of lower in/out ratios not only for their longer-distance population movements but also for their exchanges with the surrounding region. Moreover, this type of city registered below-average in/out ratios for the 'Higher managerial and professional' group for both of these components of their migration. This suggests that the two types of migration are responding to the same factors and/or they have a reinforcing effect on each other; what these analyses cannot tell us is whether this is due to an 'out-migration culture' or more simply the inexorable effect of basic factors such as economic imbalances.

Labour market factors loom large in explaining differences in migration performances

Comparing the characteristics of the weaker cities with the stronger type indicates a clear relationship with the dynamism of their economies, with the latter scoring higher on a range of labour market measures such as employment rate, local job growth and presence of graduates. Positive correlations with migration performance were also found with household income, house prices, no religion and same-sex couples. By contrast, the weaker city type featured higher levels of deprivation, down-skilling, illness, non-Whites, overcrowding, burglary and Council Tax. Similar contrasts in labour market and other characteristics exist between the cities and their surrounding regions, with the gap generally being wider for the weaker than the stronger city type, thus helping to account for the faster pace of local population deconcentration from the weaker cities.

London departs from the norm in several important respects

The London urban area can be considered to be virtually in a class of its own. This is certainly the case in terms of the massive size of its total migration flows, but is also apparent in its markedly positive relationship between in/out ratio and skill level. Its sheer strength is enough to transform the aggregate picture for Britain's large cities: the 'next largest 26 cities' have seen the continuation of the past pattern in which the higher skilled groups were more likely to be leaving the cities. Only a handful of the other large cities come close to London's level of attractiveness for the 'Higher managerial and professional' group. None of our 26 cities matches the rate at which London both receives population from overseas and sees residents departing to the rest of the UK, although in recent years Reading and Brighton have also experienced high enough rates of international immigration to be classified with it as gateway cities. London also plays a pivotal role in within-UK migration, most notably through gaining recent graduates from most other cities and losing families and older people to its own city region and beyond.

Significance of the findings

What are we to make of these observations and what implications do they have for policy? Probably the single most important conclusion to be drawn from these findings is that migration is still acting as a mechanism for supplying labour where and when it is needed. This is particularly true of the longer-distance migration that is shifting people from cities with the weaker economies to those that are the strongest, thereby helping to alleviate the joblessness of the former and reduce the bottlenecks that cause inflationary tendencies in the latter. But it also seems to apply to cities' migration exchanges with their own wider city regions, in that the prevailing centrifugal effect is shifting people into areas that have stronger economic indicators than those found in the core cities, especially for the weaker city type. This latter association is contrary to conventional wisdom that suggests that shorter-distance moves are primarily related to considerations of housing and local environment rather than job reasons. In practice, we have no way of knowing from our data whether people moving out into the rest of the city's region are commuting back to the city as opposed to taking up jobs more locally.

It also *appears* to remain the case that it is the higher skill occupations that are the more responsive to these labour market drivers. Traditionally, as shown notably by Hughes and McCormick (1987), people working in lower paid jobs tend to be relatively immobile inter-regionally, leading to much larger regional differences in unemployment rate for this group compared with that for professionals and managers. The alternative interpretation, perhaps more strongly supported by the evidence here, is that it is the migration 'signals' that are weaker for the less skilled groups. A rise in international immigration and its strong focus on London and a few other fast-growing cities seems likely to have reduced the available opportunities for lower skill people there. In any case, the UK's economic transformation from manufacturing powerhouse to a global competitor in the knowledge-based industries has placed an increasing premium on high skill workers. New growth seems just as heavily concentrated in and around London as the financial and business services that pioneered this high skill workforce growth in the capital region.

It should be acknowledged that some of the observed change in the degree to which London dominates other potential centres of the knowledge-based economy is likely to be more apparent than real. The reason is that the inclusion for the first time of moves to and from university in the census migration data in 2001 affects the analysis because the departure of people from their university cities on graduation can become confused with moves by mid-career professionals, for example. That said, we are confident that we have identified the problems that many cities have in retaining their more highly qualified people, whether they be recent graduates or not. This is a challenge that is now acknowledged much more fully than it was in the Rogers Report *Towards an urban renaissance* (Rogers Report, 1999) or the government's White Paper that followed (DETR, 2000). Indeed, it forms a major theme of the more recent report on *The state of the English cities* (Parkinson et al, 2006), building on studies that have compared the economic competitiveness of British cities with their European counterparts (notably Parkinson et al, 2004; Simmie, 2004). Moreover, individual cities – especially those in the core cities group, but many others, too – appear to be taking to heart Florida's (2002) suggestions about the importance of cities attracting and retaining highly qualified people in support of their efforts at growing the more creative components of their economies.

Given evidence on London's role as the focus of inflows of recent graduates, the results of our migration analyses make rather depressing reading. Put starkly: the very success of London in attracting highly skilled people is, in the zero-sum numbers game of internal migration, a large part of the key problem of lost talent for other cities. The analyses have shown that migration flows in and out of cities are predominantly longer distance, and for most cities flows to London make up a substantial element of the picture.

Are there some more positive aspects that policy makers can try to take advantage of? One is London's inability to retain its older residents, which at one time was seen as largely a process of retirement migration but now seems to involve all ages from around 30 and upwards (Champion and Shepherd, 2006). If the behaviour found by Fielding for the 1970s and 1980s still pertains, namely that many successful Londoners 'step off the regional escalator' before the end of their working lives, then they may move to other parts of the country (although relatively few may go far beyond the boundaries of South East England).

More generally, there is the likely effect of further demographic changes driven by the ageing population and the increasing proportion of single-person households of many different kinds. There are reasons to believe that these very gradual but deep-rooted processes may on balance favour cities by reducing the emphasis on more rural living that was particularly strong among the family-building age groups. The appearance in many cities of neighbourhoods that have become 'studentified' (Smith, 2005), along with the recent trend toward city centre living in some provincial cities (Nathan and Urwin, 2006), are both evidence of this set of processes. That said, it should be noted that the regression analyses showed that the highly skilled groups tended not to be attracted to areas with many students.

Turning finally to the implications of this report's evidence on migration flows within city regions, we have found relatively little to challenge the received wisdom that informs the policies of planners and city managers. So far as the three case study city regions provide findings of wider consequence, the main interest will probably be in the fact that migration flows are not strongly increasing social segregation between localities. The tightness of the London housing market can produce the more radical shifts familiar as gentrification and here the evidence was that the 'Higher managerial and professional' group were moving into areas where they had not previously been numerous (although it is possible that this is largely due to newly arriving graduates finding a first base in one of the capital's less advantaged areas). More generally, it is probable that social segmentation is largely the cumulative effect of many people trying over time to 'move up the housing ladder' and the vast majority of these flows are short-distance moves taking place within localities and so not included in the analyses reported here.

Society is becoming dominated by increasing mobility, and migration is the physical expression of a longer-term form of mobility. Yet the limits on mobility mean that some groups in society have very narrow horizons still: the data analysed here could not measure mobility rates, but it did suggest that the less skilled were the least likely to move to more economically prosperous areas. Policies such as the housing provision for key workers in London are clearly only the start of what could be a much wider response to this problem of restricted mobility. At the same time, dispersing growth away from the London region looks like a 'win-win' situation by reducing pressure on the South East and also addressing the chronic economic imbalances across the country.

References

Bailey, N. and Livingston, M. (2007) *Population turnover and area deprivation*, Bristol/York: The Policy Press/Joseph Rowntree Foundation.

Bramley, G., Pawson, H. and Third, H. (2000) *Low demand and unpopular housing*, London: DETR.

Brunsdon, C., Coombes, M., Munro, M. and Symon, P. (1991) 'Housing and labour market interactions: an analysis of house price inflation in British LLMAs, 1988/87', in M. Satsangi (ed) *Changing housing finance systems*, Studies in Housing No 3, Glasgow: Centre for Housing Research, University of Glasgow, pp 230-70.

Bulusu, L. (1991) *A review of migration data sources*, OPCS Occasional Paper 39, London: Office of Population Censuses and Surveys.

Champion, T (2001) 'Urbanisation, suburbanisation, counterurbanisation and reurbanisation', in R. Paddison (ed) *Handbook of urban studies*, London: Sage Publications, pp 143-61.

Champion, T. (2002) *The containment of urban Britain: Retrospect and prospect*, Milan: FrancoAngeli.

Champion, T. (2004) 'The Census and the cities', *Town & Country Planning*, vol 73, no 1, pp 20-2.

Champion, T. (2005) 'Population movement within the UK', in R. Chappell (ed) *Focus on people and migration*, Houndmills: Palgrave Macmillan for ONS, pp 91-113.

Champion, T. and Fisher, T. (2003) 'The social selectivity of migration flows affecting Britain's larger conurbations: an analysis of the 1991 Census Regional Migration Tables', *Scottish Geographical Journal*, vol 119, no 3, pp 229-46.

Champion, T. and Fisher, T. (2004) 'Migration, residential preferences and the changing environment of cities', in M. Boddy and M. Parkinson (eds) *City matters: Competitiveness, cohesion and urban governance*, Bristol: The Policy Press, pp 111-28.

Champion, T. and Shepherd, J. (2006) 'Demographic change in rural England', in P. Lowe and L. Speakman (eds) *The ageing countryside: The growing older population of rural England*, London: Age Concern England, pp 29-50.

Champion, T., Atkins, D., Coombes, M. and Fotheringham, S. (1998b) *Urban exodus*, London: Council for the Protection of Rural England.

Champion, T., Fotheringham, S., Rees, P., Boyle, P. and Stillwell, J. (1998a) *The determinants of migration flows in England: A review of existing data and evidence*, Newcastle upon Tyne: Department of Geography, University of Newcastle upon Tyne.

Coombes, M. (2002) 'Localities and city regions codebook', in P. Rees, D. Martin and P. Williamson (eds) *The census data system*, CDS resource 5, Chichester: Wiley.

Coombes, M. and Charlton, M. (1992) 'Flows to and from London: a decade of change?', in J. Stillwell, P. Rees and P. Boden (eds) *Migration processes and patterns, Volume 2: Population redistribution in the United Kingdom*, London: Belhaven Press, pp 56-77.

Coombes, M. and Raybould, S. (2004) 'Finding work in 2001: urban-rural contrasts across England in employment rates and job availability', *Area*, vol 36, pp 202-22.

DETR (Department of the Environment, Transport and the Regions) (2000) *Our towns and cities: The future. Towards an urban renaissance*, London: DETR.

Dorling, D., Ballas, D., Thomas, B. and Pritchard, J. (2004) *Pilot mapping of local social polarisation in three areas in England 1971–2001*, Sheffield: University of Sheffield (sasi.group.sheffield.ac.uk/publications/2004/pilot_mapping_tech_report.doc).

Fielding, A.J. (1992) 'Migration and social mobility: South East England as an "escalator" region', *Regional Studies*, vol 26, pp 1-15.

Fielding, A.J. (1993) 'Migration and the metropolis', *Progress in Planning*, vol 39, pp 71-166.

Florida, R. (2002) *The rise of the creative class*, New York, NY: Basic Books.

Geyer, H. and Kontuly, T. (1993) 'A theoretical foundation for the concept of differential urbanisation', *International Regional Science Review*, vol 15, pp 157-77.

GLA (Greater London Authority) Economics (2004) *World city, world knowledge: The economic contribution of London's higher education sector*, London: GLA.

Hall, P., Thomas, R., Gracey, H. and Drewett, R. (1973) *The containment of urban England*, London: George Allen and Unwin.

Hickman, P., Robinson, D., Casey, R., Green, S. and Powell, R. (2007) *Understanding housing demand: Learning from rising markets in Yorkshire and the Humber*, Coventry: Chartered Institute of Housing.

HM Treasury, DTI (Department of Trade and Industry) and ODPM (Office of the Deputy Prime Minister) (2006) *Devolving decision making: 3 – Meeting the regional economic challenge: The importance of cities to regional growth*, London: HM Treasury.

Hughes, G.A. and McCormick, B. (1987) 'Housing markets, unemployment and labour market flexibility in the UK', *European Economic Review*, pp 615-45.

Klaassen, L.H., Molle, W.T.W and Paelinck, J.H.P. (1981) *Dynamics of urban development*, Aldershot: Gower.

Nathan, M. and Urwin, C. (2006) *City people: City centre living in the UK*, London: IPPR Centre for Cities.

Parkinson, M., Hutchins, M., Simmie, J., Clark, G. and Verdonk, H. (2004) *Competitive European cities: Where do the core cities stand?*, London: ODPM.

Parkinson, M. et al (2006) *The state of the English cities: A research study*, London: ODPM.

Perry, R., Dean, K. and Brown, B. (1986) *Counterurbanisation: Case studies of urban to rural movement*, Norwich: GeoBooks.

Rees, P. (1998) 'What do you want from the 2001 Census? Results of an ESRC/JISC survey of user views', *Environment and Planning A*, vol 30, no 10, pp 1775-96.

Rees, P., Thomas, F. and Duke-Williams, O. (2002) 'Migration data from the census', in P. Rees, D. Martin and P. Williamson (eds) *The census data system*, Chichester: Wiley, pp 245-67.

Rogers Report (1999) *Towards an urban renaissance*, Final report of the Urban Task Force, London: DETR.

Scottish Executive (2004) *Background analysis to the framework for economic development in Scotland*, Edinburgh: Scottish Executive (www.scotland.gov.uk/Publications/2004/09/19882/42513).

SEU (Social Exclusion Unit) (1998) *Bringing Britain together: A national strategy for neighbourhood renewal*, London: SEU.

Simmie, J. (2004) 'Innovation clusters and competitive cities in the UK and Europe', in M. Boddy and M. Parkinson (eds) *City matters: Competitiveness, cohesion and urban governance*, Bristol The: Policy Press, pp 171-96.

Smith, D.P. (2005) '"Studentification": the gentrification factory?', in R. Atkinson and G. Bridge (eds) *The new urban colonialism: Gentrification in a global context*, London: Routledge, pp 72-89.

Stillwell, J. and Duke-Williams, O. (2007) 'Understanding the 2001 Census migration and commuting data: the impact of small cell adjustment and problems of comparison with 1991', *Journal of the Royal Statistical Society: Series A (Statistics in Society)*, vol 170, no 2, pp 425-45.

Williams, M. and Champion, T. (1998) 'Cornwall, poverty and in-migration', *Cornish Studies Second Series*, vol 6, pp 118-26.

A

Appendix: The 2001 Census special migration statistics

The analyses undertaken for this study have been based entirely on the 2001 Census Special Migration Statistics Set 1 (SMS1). This dataset provides counts of migrants and 'moving groups of migrants in households' changing address in the 12 months before census day between each lower-tier local authority and every other one. The use of this district-to-district migration matrix is necessitated by defining cities in terms of groupings of districts, so that the moves taking place between the constituent districts of any one city must be excluded from the counts of that city's total inflows and outflows. The SMS1 tables also contain counts of migrants who indicated that they had had 'no usual address' one year ago, but these have to be excluded from the study because these are people whose address one year ago is not known. Also, migrants who were living at an address outside the UK one year ago are not analysed here, because by definition there is no comparable data on international outflows in the UK census to allow a comparison of inflows and outflows.

Table MG109

The main part of the migration analysis for this study was undertaken on SMS1 Table MG109. This provides counts of heads of 'moving groups' (one or more people moving from the same previous address) by National Statistics Socioeconomic Classification (NS-SEC), further disaggregated by gender and type and size of moving group. The whole table takes the form shown in Table A1.

There are three separate panels to this table: for all moving group reference persons (MGRPs), male MGRPs, and female MGRPs. Attention has been focused on a single count of all heads by NS-SEC, not only combining male and female but also summing wholly moving households and other moving groups and ignoring size of moving group. This is because the counts to be analysed are just for the one person in each moving group who has been classified.

For the purposes of the study, the NS-SEC categories have been collapsed into six groups. As described in the text, the eight occupationally based categories from 1.1 through to 7 have been aggregated into four categories: 'Higher managerial and professional' (1.1 and 1.2), 'Lower managerial and professional' (2), 'Intermediate' (3 and 4) and 'Lower' (5-7). These represent clearly separate levels of labour market skills and social status. Of the remaining three categories, MGRPs who were in 'Full-time study' at the census have been kept separate because of both their particular interest for the study of human capital and their very distinctive migration patterns. The other two groups have been combined on advice from the census agencies because of mistakes in the classification process that meant that some members of one category were wrongly placed in the other.

Table A1: Format of SMS1 Table MG109

NS-SEC of reference person of moving group	Wholly moving households				Other moving groups			
	All	1p	2p	3+p	All	1p	2p	3+p
Total								
1.1 Large employers and higher managerial occupations								
1.2 Higher professional occupations								
2 Lower managerial and professional occupations								
3 Intermediate occupations								
4 Small employers and own account workers								
5 Lower supervisory and technical occupations								
6 Semi-routine occupations								
7 Routine occupations								
Never worked and long-term unemployed								
Full-time student								
Not classifiable for other reasons (eg aged 75+)								

Note: p = person.

Methodological issues

The research has had to operate within the limitations of the data provided by the census authorities.

Most notably, there are several data issues. These include:

Coverage of the population: the One Number Census process imputed records for some 6% of UK residents that were estimated not to have appeared on a census form. Even so, the latest population estimates suggest that, even after this, the census omitted some 0.25 million residents and, necessarily, so too does this study.

Coverage of migration for the enumerated population: judging by the evidence of previous censuses (this aspect of data quality was not checked in a post-enumeration survey in the 2001 Census), a not insignificant proportion of migrants (perhaps 10%) will not have declared themselves to be such, and this may be a biased share.

Quality of answers to the 'change of address' question: people who indicated that they were migrants but gave inadequate details of their previous address had the latter imputed. There is no information available on how reliable this imputation will have been.

No usual address one year ago: in the 2001 Census for the first time a migrant was allowed to tick a box if they considered that 12 months earlier they had no address that they could call their usual address. Some 0.45 million people or over 6% of migrant residents indicated this. As they were not asked their whereabouts at that time, it is not known which area had lost them as a result of their subsequent move, not even whether they were inside or outside the UK. As mentioned above, these could not be included in the analysis of cities' inflows and outflows.

Effect of disclosure controls: all census data is subject to a degree of data modification to ensure that users will not be able to positively identify a real individual in the population. In the 2001 Census this modification included (for people enumerated in England, Wales and Northern Ireland, but not Scotland) an extra element of data perturbation termed 'small cell adjustment'. This involved recoding any non-total cell count that was originally 1 and 2 into 0 or 3, although not necessarily rounding to the nearest, with all marginal totals being the sum of the recoded data. Since the vast majority of cell counts in the SMS were expected (from the experience of previous censuses) to be 0, 1 or 2, this step will have significantly altered this dataset for all flows except those ending in Scotland. In particular, there is no way of telling which zeros in the modified dataset are actual zeros as opposed to 1s and 2s recoded to 0. The hope is that, if enough cells and zones are summed, this will produce something close to the figure that would have been produced by summing the original data, but tests by Stillwell and Duke-Williams (2007) indicate that there is a significant downward bias. Unfortunately, there is no way of allowing for this when interpreting the results of our analyses.

Besides these general data issues, there are two other issues that are especially relevant to this analysis of the socioeconomic characteristics of migrants. One is that census data do not allow the calculation of the true net effect of migration on the composition of the population of a place. Because address one year ago is the only retrospective question asked, the only details about people one year ago that one can be highly confident about are those that, to all intents and purposes, can be deemed not to change (for example, gender, ethnicity) and those that change predictably (for example, age). Unfortunately, labour market position and occupation (the main ingredients of NS-SEC) are among the characteristics that are most likely to change with a change of address, although not as much as housing and household characteristics.

What it is possible to do is to compare the after-move characteristics of people moving in one direction (for example, into a particular city) with those of people moving in the opposite direction (for example, out of that city). Subtracting one from the other to give a net change figure, however, is valid only on the assumption of no change between before and after the move or if that characteristic would have changed in that manner anyway even if they had not moved. Perhaps the most problematic element of NS-SEC in this context is 'Full-time students', particularly given that in the 2001 Census (for the first time) migration is defined to include moves of students from parental home to term-time residence and moves of graduates from term-time residence to post-university destination (as well as accommodation changes while at university). For university cities, migrants classified by NS-SEC are bound to show a much higher representation of students in their inflows than in their outflows, because students who graduated in the pre-census year and changed address will not be classified as students (unless proceeding to postgraduate or other full-time education). The results of analyses using NS-SEC have needed to be interpreted in the light of this.

The other issue is the impossibility of making an accurate and meaningful study of the changes that have taken place between migration in the pre-census year in 2001 and that in the equivalent period before previous censuses. The change in the definition of student's usual address, by itself, rules out valid comparisons across censuses, let alone the effects of differences in census coverage, in the treatment of 'no origin stated' and 'no usual address one year ago' and in the type of disclosure control used. Additionally, NS-SEC is a new variable that is considerably different from the 20-fold Socioeconomic Group (SEG) classification used to classify migrants in the 1981 and 1991 Censuses. Also relevant are the changes in local government areas in the mid-1990s, and the fact that the stage of the economic cycle in 1990-91 (a period of deep national recession and low migration levels) provided a very different context from that in 2000-01 (period of strong economic growth and high migration levels).

Despite all these caveats, the census data on migration is the best available for the purposes of this study. This is especially in terms of the geographical detail it gives about the origin and destinations of moves and in terms of the information collected about the characteristics of migrants, albeit only after their change of address. The key challenge is to try and allow as far as possible for the special conceptual and quality features and thereby be in a position to be able to assess the level of confidence to be placed in the findings.

B

Appendix: Selecting the cities for the study

There were two main criteria used in selecting cities: 2001 population size of the urban area, and identification as the principal city of one of the 43 CURDS (Centre for Urban and Regional Development Studies) city regions (Coombes, 2002).

The use of physically built-up areas, rather than administrative cities, is essential to allow a much more consistent comparison of one city with another. We followed Parkinson et al (2006) in using primary urban areas (PUAs): these are based on the built-up areas defined for the 2001 Census but split apart any cities like Leeds and Bradford with just a tangential physical link and which are in separate labour market areas (as defined by travel-to-work areas).

The rationale for the size cut-off was mainly prompted by the study's emphasis on larger cities, given their being the primary focus of government policy in both urban regeneration and social exclusion arenas. After looking at the distribution of cities by the 2001 Census population size of their PUAs and whether or not they were the centre of one of the CURDS city regions, a size cut-off of 195,000 was selected. Below this, there is a big margin before the next qualifying city-region centres: Ipswich (146,000) and Oxford (145,000), with York smaller again at 134,000. This gave a total of 27 cities (as shown in Map 3.1).

In practice, data availability – both on migration from the 2001 Census special migration statistics (SMS) (see Appendix A) and on some of the explanatory variables (see Appendix D) – made it advisable to use the best fit of district and unitary local government areas to PUAs. Most cities were aggregates of two or more districts. London is by far the largest on this PUA basis, comprising not only the 'square mile' administered by the City of London Corporation and the 32 London boroughs but also a further 13 districts beyond the Greater London Authority (GLA) boundary in Essex, Hertfordshire, Kent and Surrey. Nine of the 27 cities, however, were best approximated by a single local authority, either because they were contained fully within it (as in the case of Leeds) or because the part of the urban area in the surrounding district made up only a small proportion of the latter's total population (as in the case of the East Riding of Yorkshire in relation to Hull).

The criterion that the cities should be the centres of city regions was linked to the intention of distinguishing the part of the PUA's migration exchanges that were shorter distances moves to and from the surrounding area (see Chapter 5) from those that were with the rest of the country (see Chapter 4). In addition, the city region forms the geographical basis of the three case studies (see Chapter 5 and Appendix E).

The composition of the cities, in terms of the local authority areas making up their PUAs (in **bold**) and the remainder of their city regions, is given in Table B1.

Table B1: The 27 PUAs and city regions: composition in terms of a best-fit by local authority areas

Note: Areas in **bold** are in the PUA of the city region's principal city

BIRMINGHAM
Birmingham
Bromsgrove
Cannock Chase
Dudley
Lichfield
Redditch
Sandwell
Solihull
South Staffordshire
Tamworth
Walsall
Wolverhampton
Wyre Forest

BRADFORD
Bradford
Craven

BRIGHTON
Adur
Brighton and Hove
Eastbourne
Hastings
Lewes
Rother
Wealden
Worthing

BRISTOL
Bath & North East Somerset
Bristol
Kennet
Mendip
North Somerset
Sedgemoor
South Gloucestershire
South Somerset
Taunton Deane
West Somerset
West Wiltshire

CARDIFF
Blaenau Gwent
Bridgend
Caerphilly
Cardiff
Merthyr Tydfil
Monmouthshire
Newport
Rhondda; Cynon; Taff
Vale of Glamorgan
Torfaen

COVENTRY
Coventry
North Warwickshire
Nuneaton and Bedworth
Rugby
Stratford-on-Avon
Warwick

DERBY
Derby
Derbyshire Dales
East Staffordshire
South Derbyshire

EDINBURGH
Berwick-upon-Tweed
Clackmannanshire
East Lothian
Falkirk
Fife
Edinburgh
Midlothian
Scottish Borders
Stirling
West Lothian

GLASGOW
Argyll & Bute
East Ayrshire
East Dunbartonshire
East Renfrewshire
Glasgow
Inverclyde
North Ayrshire
North Lanarkshire
Renfrewshire
South Ayrshire
South Lanarkshire
West Dunbartonshire

HULL
East Riding of Yorkshire
Kingston upon Hull
North East Lincolnshire
North Lincolnshire

LEEDS
Calderdale
Harrogate
Kirklees
Leeds
Wakefield

LEICESTER
Blaby
Charnwood
Harborough
Hinckley and Bosworth
Leicester
Melton
North West Leicestershire
Oadby and Wigston
Rutland

LIVERPOOL
Halton
Knowsley
Liverpool
Sefton
St. Helens
West Lancashire
Wirral

LONDON
Ashford
Barking and Dagenham
Barnet
Basildon
Bedford
Bexley
Braintree
Brent
Brentwood
Bromley
Broxbourne
Camden
Canterbury
Castle Point
Chelmsford
City of London
Colchester
Crawley
Croydon
Dacorum
Dartford
Dover
Ealing
East Hampshire
East Hertfordshire
Elmbridge
Enfield
Epping Forest
Epsom and Ewell
Gravesham
Greenwich
Guildford
Hackney
Hammersmith and Fulham
Haringey
Harlow
Harrow
Hart
Havering
Hertsmere
Hillingdon
Horsham
Hounslow
Islington
Kensington and Chelsea
Kingston upon Thames
Lambeth
Lewisham
Luton
Maidstone
Maldon
Medway
Merton
Mid Bedfordshire
Mid Sussex
Milton Keynes
Mole Valley
Newham
North Hertfordshire
Redbridge
Reigate and Banstead
Richmond upon Thames
Rochford
Runnymede
Rushmoor
Sevenoaks
Shepway
South Bedfordshire
Southend-on-Sea
Southwark
Spelthorne
St. Albans
Stevenage
Surrey Heath
Sutton
Swale
Tandridge
Tendring
Thanet
Three Rivers
Thurrock
Tonbridge and Malling
Tower Hamlets
Tunbridge Wells
Uttlesford
Waltham Forest
Wandsworth
Watford
Waverley
Welwyn Hatfield
Westminster
Woking

MANCHESTER
Bolton
Bury
High Peak
Macclesfield
Manchester
Oldham
Rochdale
Rossendale
Salford
Stockport
Tameside
Trafford
Vale Royal
Warrington
Wigan

MIDDLESBROUGH
Darlington
Hambleton
Hartlepool
Middlesbrough
Redcar and Cleveland
Richmondshire
Sedgefield
Stockton-on-Tees
Teesdale
Wear Valley

NEWCASTLE
Alnwick
Blyth Valley
Castle Morpeth
Chester-le-Street
Derwentside
Durham
Easington
Gateshead
Newcastle upon Tyne
North Tyneside
South Tyneside
Sunderland
Tynedale
Wansbeck

NORTHAMPTON
Corby
Daventry
East Northamptonshire
Kettering
Northampton
South Northamptonshire
Wellingborough

NORWICH
Breckland
Broadland
Forest Heath
Great Yarmouth
King's Lynn and West Norfolk
North Norfolk
Norwich
South Norfolk
Waveney

NOTTINGHAM
Amber Valley
Ashfield
Broxtowe
Erewash
Gedling
Mansfield
Newark and Sherwood
Nottingham
Rushcliffe
South Kesteven

PLYMOUTH
Caradon
Carrick
Isles of Scilly
Kerrier
North Cornwall
Penwith
Plymouth
Restormel
South Hams
Teignbridge
Torbay
West Devon

PORTSMOUTH
Arun
Chichester
Fareham
Gosport
Havant
Isle of Wight
Portsmouth

PRESTON
Barrow-in-Furness
Blackburn with Darwen
Blackpool
Burnley
Chorley
Fylde
Hyndburn
Lancaster
Pendle
Preston
Ribble Valley
South Lakeland
South Ribble
Wyre

READING
Aylesbury Vale
Basingstoke and Deane
Bracknell Forest
Chiltern
Reading
Slough
South Bucks
West Berkshire
Windsor and Maidenhead
Wokingham
Wycombe

SHEFFIELD
Barnsley
Bassetlaw
Bolsover
Chesterfield
Doncaster
North East Derbyshire
Rotherham
Sheffield

SOUTHAMPTON
Bournemouth
Christchurch
East Dorset
Eastleigh
New Forest
North Dorset
Poole
Purbeck
Salisbury
Southampton
Test Valley
West Dorset
Weymouth and Portland
Winchester

STOKE
Congleton
Crewe and Nantwich
Newcastle-under-Lyme
Stafford
Staffordshire Moorlands
Stoke-on-Trent

C

Appendix: Classifying the 27 cities

A classification of cities was required in order to summarise the main features of the cities' migration exchanges, especially those with the rest of the UK beyond their city region boundaries (see Chapter 4). This appendix describes the thinking behind the four-fold typology that we developed for this purpose.

One potential complication in interpreting the analysis of migration patterns within Britain is the major influence that international migration has on the within-UK migration of particular areas (see, for instance, Figure 2.3). Where there are large flows of immigrants in particular, the possible consequences include a potential displacement of in-migrants from other parts of Britain and a high degree of 'spillover' of out-migrants to adjacent areas owing to the strong pressure on housing markets. As a result, it is important to identify whether any cities are 'outliers' in the scale of their international migration flows.

Table C1 shows the five of the 27 cities selected for this study that recorded the highest levels of international immigration in 2001-03, based on the number who arrived during that 24-month period as a percentage of the cities' 2001 total populations. London's value is particularly high, but those for Reading and Brighton also represent an annual average infusion to their populations from this source of at least 1%. We take this level – admittedly, rather arbitrarily – as being that where international immigration is likely to have large consequences for intra-national migration. These three cities may play a similar role to the US cities that are identified as gateway cities for immigrants, so we label these three cities (and their wider city regions) collectively as the gateway type.

Table C1: International immigrants as a % of 2001 population: top five cities (2001-03)

City	%
London	3.51
Reading	2.36
Brighton	2.13
Coventry	1.96
Bristol	1.86

Turning to the remaining 24 cities, the decision was taken to classify these into three equal membership types based on the strength of their migration balances with the rest of the UK beyond their city region boundaries. That component of their migration exchanges was chosen because of the major concern of the study being with whether cities are losing human capital, and migrants who move only out to areas in the rest of the city region may commute back and thus still be part of the labour force of the city.

The approach taken to placing the 24 cities into three types was based on ranking them on their in/out ratios for three categories of moving group reference persons (MGRPs):

- 'Higher managerial and professional' MGRPs, being the highly-skilled group and the major interest of this study

- 'Low skill' MGRPs, being the least skilled group and the one whose members are least likely to migrate
- 'All' MGRPs, comprising all the recorded moving groups including students and those who were not classified occupationally in the census.

The logic of this approach is that it places greatest emphasis on the 'Higher managerial and professional' and the 'Low skill' groups, because they are included both as separate categories and in the aggregate counts. While this study is pre-eminently interested in the former, the fact that 'Low skill' people are the least likely to migrate the longer distances that are analysed here makes it all the more notable if a city has an in/out ratio for this group that is very different to that of the other cities.

Table C2 shows the rankings, on each of these three migration categories, of the 24 remaining cities, with the city with the highest in/out ratio being ranked 1 in each case. The final column shows a sum of the rank values for each city and the cities are listed in ascending order of this summary value, with the split into three groups of eight cities indicated by the black lines. These are termed, respectively, the stronger, moderate and weaker types (see Table 4.3, Chapter 4).

Table C2: Rankings on in/out ratios of 24 cities for migration exchanges with the rest of the UK beyond their city region boundaries

	Higher M&P	Low skill	All MGRPs	Sum
Edinburgh	3	1	2	6
Bristol	5	7	3	15
Preston	9	2	4	15
Portsmouth	10	4	5	19
Leeds	6	14	1	21
Norwich	7	6	12	25
Northampton	2	15	10	27
Derby	1	10	17	28
Manchester	4	16	11	31
Nottingham	20	5	6	31
Plymouth	14	9	9	32
Bradford	11	3	18	32
Glasgow	13	11	13	37
Newcastle	16	19	8	43
Southampton	8	21	15	44
Sheffield	22	18	7	47
Coventry	24	8	16	48
Leicester	18	13	20	51
Cardiff	15	23	14	52
Birmingham	12	20	22	54
Hull	21	12	21	54
Middlesbrough	19	17	19	55
Liverpool	17	24	24	65
Stoke	23	22	23	68

D

Appendix: List of 'explanatory' variables

Affordability: affordability (average weekly household income 1998 divided by average price of semi-detached house 2000/01)
Commuting 10km(+): % in employment commuting 10km or more
Council Tax: Band D (£) in 1998 (used for London only)
Council renting: % households renting from local authority
Crime: Index of Multiple Deprivation (IMD) 2004 crime indicator
Degree: % 16- to 74-year-olds with degree
Detached and semi-detached: % dwellings detached/semi-detached
Down-skilling: % point change in proportion of 'manual' households 1991-2001
Employment rate change: % point change in employment rate 1991-2001
Employment rate: % 16- to 74-year-olds in work (employed and self-employed)
Ethnic diversification: % point change in proportion of non-Whites 1991-2001
Flat price: average price of flat 2000
Green space: % area in green space
HA renting: % households renting from housing association (HA) and other social besides council
'Higher M&P' skill group: % classified persons in 'Higher managerial and professional' occupations
Housebuilding: annual average house completions 1997-2001 (Bailey and Livingston, 2006) per 100 dwellings (used for London only)
Household income: Office for National Statistics (ONS) modelled estimate of area average weekly household income (£) 1998
Infant mortality rate: deaths under one year of age per 1,000 live births, 2001 (used for London only)
'Intermediate skill' group: % classified persons in intermediate occupations
Job accessibility: job accessibility (Coombes and Raybould, 2004)
Limiting long-term illness: % with limiting long-term illness
Local job growth: job accessibility change 1991-2001 (Coombes and Raybould, 2004)
Lone-parent families: % households with lone-parent family
Lone pensioners: % households with pensioner living alone
'Low skill' group: % classified persons in low occupations
'Lower M&P skill' group: % classified persons in 'Lower managerial and professional' occupations
Manual households: % households with 'manual' social grade
Migrant residents: % residents who had changed address in 12 months before the census (including those living outside the UK and those with no usual address one year ago)
No qualifications: % 16- to 74-year-olds with no qualifications

No religion: % people indicating 'no religion'
No usual address one year ago: migrant residents with 'no usual address' 12 months before the census as % of all residents 2001
Non-Whites: % not White
Owner-occupation: % households owner-occupied
Privately renting: % households renting privately
Recent immigrants: % residents who had been living outside the UK 12 months before the census
Semi-detached price change: % change in average price of semi-detached house 1995/96-2000/01
Semi-detached price: average price of semi-detached house 2000
Social grade AB: % households in social grade AB
Students: % full-time students
Turnover index: total numbers of people entering and leaving addresses (known within-UK moves only) 2000-01 as % of residents
Under 16: % residents aged under 16
Unoccupied dwellings: % dwellings unoccupied

Notes:

Variables refer to 2001 unless a different date or dates is stated in the list above.

The denominator used for ratios is all residents, unless an alternative base is specified.

Variables such as the Council Tax indicator were calculated as population-weighted averages of the values of the constituent areas.

Most of the variables derive, at least in part, from 2001 Census of population datasets; the other sources used were provided by the ONS (regional trends and neighbourhood statistics) or the Department for Communities and Local Government (housing statistics and the state of the cities database), except where an alternative source is referenced in the variable list.

E

Appendix: Selecting the three case study cities

Resources permitted the more detailed examination of three cities. Even in the earliest stages of the work, it became obvious that one of these should be London. Its huge size and well-documented importance in UK migration patterns had more or less determined its choice, but this view was amply confirmed by the finding that London was highly distinctive in terms of the nature of its migration linkages with other parts of the country and the unusual nature of its positive relationship between in/out ratio and skill level. This appendix therefore explains how the other two cities – Birmingham and Bristol – came to be selected.

Size was seen as a key criterion. Larger cities tend to be more interesting simply because what happens there affects more people. In addition, smaller cities more often have characteristics that are unique to themselves, which means that evidence about their experience provides little guidance on what is happening in other cities. That said and while having already selected the largest city of all, it seemed valuable for the two case study cities to be of rather different size.

Level of economic prosperity and broad regional location formed a second key criterion. This would allow a comparison to be drawn between a provincial city with a strong economy and tight housing market and one with a weaker economy and signs of low demand. Given the attention given to the North/South divide in recent years, one should be selected from each side of the North/South boundary, which, since the early 1980s recession, has been seen to run roughly from the Severn estuary to the Wash or – in terms of Government Office Regions – to follow the boundary between the East Midlands (in the South) and the West Midlands (in the North).

The boundaries of the cities were a further consideration. While the 27 city analyses used definitions of cities and city regions that form the 'best fit' possible from the whole local authorities, the degree of fit varied somewhat between cities. At least some of the analyses for these two case study cities were to use ward-based data that, of course, offers greater boundary precision. The issue here is that, for any region where the 'best fit' is not a close match to the ward-based boundaries, the overall results for a case study area may be markedly different for those analyses where the results from two phases can be directly compared. To avoid this problem, preference is given to those cities and city regions for which there is little difference between the local authority-based 'best fit' boundaries and the ward-based boundaries.

In addition, the concerns about the effects of students on the migration data (see Chapter 4) suggest that there would be an advantage if at least one of the case studies was a city region where the migration flows are less likely to be 'dominated' by people moving for the purposes of study and at the end of their courses.

Finally, the two cities were chosen to be different in relation to their observed migration patterns. The most significant distinction for the purposes of this study was their overall migration performance and the relationship between in/out ratio and skill level. One should therefore be chosen from the list of stronger cities in Table 4.3 (see also Appendix C) and one from the list of weaker cities. Moreover, given that London displays a strong positive relationship between in/out ratio and skill level, it was deemed best if one of the other two should have a strongly negative relationship and the other a less marked gradient in either direction.

The combination of factors outlined above, including the North/South dimension, makes it clear that the larger city case study should be one of the conurbations' principal cities. Of these, Birmingham has a close 'best fit' between the local authority- and ward-based boundaries. It is also the one where the student effect is unlikely to be so great and, in terms of its migration profile, is characterised by substantial migration loss and a negative relationship between in/out ratio and social status. Among the southern cities in the stronger city type, Bristol is the largest (without duplicating Birmingham in size terms) and one of the more prosperous; it also has one of the closest local authority-based 'best fits' and its migration flows are not simply dominated by the influence of any single factor like students or the influence of London. It also has no clear relationship between in/out ratio and social status.

The final step was to define zones, or 'localities', for the analysis of between-place migration within each of the three case study city regions. Our idea here was that there should be a roughly similar number of localities in each of the case study regions, so as to maximise the comparability between them despite the very large differences between their populations. It was also felt that the analyses would not be readily interpretable if there were as many as 100 localities for which separate results were mapped or tabulated. Of these localities, the bulk should be in the central city because there is greater interest in the pattern of migration there. Finally, there is a clear benefit of comparability if the localities are of roughly similar population size, or at least if those within the city itself are similar to each other and those in the rest of the region are also similar to each other.

The main data for the case study analyses was available at the ward level, although if any localities are defined at the local authority level then their analyses can, at least potentially, use the additional data available at that wider scale. One disadvantage of using individual 2001 wards as localities, however, is that this makes it difficult to link 1991 data into the analyses when deriving variables measuring change over time. In fact, using wards would mean that there would be an unmanageable number of localities even for the smallest case study region (Bristol). Therefore, it was decided that the smallest areas that should be used as localities were the *tracts* that have been defined by the team led by Danny Dorling (and used in previous work for the Joseph Rowntree Foundation). The tracts are of a fairly consistent population size – between 30,000 and 50,000 in most cases – and were defined as groupings of 2001 Census wards that closely match groupings of the wards for which 1991 Census data can be obtained. For London and the non-PUA part of Birmingham, however, whole local authorities or groupings of these would provide sufficient geographical detail for our purposes.

The considerations set out above led to the locality definitions shown in Table E1.

Table E1: Localities in the three case study city regions

City region and component	Number of localities	Basis of localities	Remarks
London	46		
City (PUA)	36	Individual local authorities	Except that City of London and Westminster are combined, as are sets of local authorities outside the GLA area
Rest of city region	10	Grouped local authorities	Except for Milton Keynes local authority
Birmingham	60		
City (PUA)	52	Individual tracts	
Rest of city region	8	Individual local authorities	
Bristol	34		
City (PUA)	12	Individual tracts	
Rest of city region	22	Individual tracts	

Note: PUA = Primary Urban Area

F

Appendix: Correlation and reduction of the explanatory variables

This appendix first presents the results of correlations analyses at the locality level between the in/out ratios for 'Higher managerial and professional' MGRPs and the full set of explanatory variables. This leads to the decision on which of these variables to select for the regression analyses, at the same level, which are presented in the main report (Chapter 5).

Table F1 lists all of the characteristics that are significantly correlated (down to 5%) with the 'Higher managerial and professional' group's in/out ratios for the 46 localities of London's city region. There are just six of these. The strongest association is a positive one with the rate of housebuilding, which by itself 'explains' (in the statistical sense, that is R^2) 22% of the overall variance in the in/out ratios of this group across the localities. Looking further down the list, it is found that the localities that registered the highest in/out ratios for this high status group in the year before the 2001 Census were also those with the highest levels of green space and people expressing no religious affiliation and with the fewest people born outside the UK, living in privately rented housing and suffering from a limiting long-term illness. These are all characteristics that are likely to be associated with more middle-class residents, although this cannot be a simple underlying explanation because social structure variables did not emerge from the analysis as strong influences in their own right.

Table F1: Statistically significant correlations between 'Higher managerial and professional' MGRPs' within-region migration and the characteristics of the 46 localities of London's city region

Zone characteristic	*r*
Housebuilding	+0.469
No religion	+0.350
Born outside the UK	–0.322
Privately renting	–0.313
Limiting long-term illness	–0.302
Green space	+0.299

Note: The dependent variable is the in/out ratio logged; r of 0.377 and above is significant at 1% level, 0.291 at 5%. Only variables significant down to 5% are listed. See Appendix D for the full specification and source of the characteristics.

Source: The dependent variable is calculated from the 2001 Census special migration statistics (SMS), Table MG109. Crown copyright

Repeating the same exercise for the 60 localities of Birmingham's city region produces a much longer list of statistically significant correlations. Table F2 merely gives a feel for the most highly associated characteristics by listing the top 10. The localities with the highest in/out ratios for 'Higher managerial and professional' MGRPs are those with the highest levels of residents commuting long distance, working-age people in employment, households classified as social grade A or B, average household income, land not built over and people in 'Lower managerial and professional' occupations (although not the 'Higher' group as already seen from Table 4.5). These localities are also characterised by the fewest 16- to 17-years-olds without qualifications, the fewest manual households, the fewest migrants that were homeless the year before, and the lowest crime rate. In the Birmingham case then, the middle-class effect can be observed both directly and also indirectly through associated variables such as the higher level of green space.

Table F2: Highest 10 correlations between 'Higher managerial and professional' MGRPs' within-region migration and the characteristics of the 60 localities of Birmingham's city region

Locality characteristic	r
Commuting 10km(+)	+0.477
No qualifications	-0.456
Employment rate	+0.455
Manual households	-0.453
'Lower managerial and professional' group	+0.443
Social grade AB	+0.437
Green space	+0.436
No usual address one year ago	-0.436
Crime	-0.425
Household income	+0.416

Note: The dependent variable is the in/out ratio logged; r of 0.329 and above is significant at 1% level. Only the 10 highest correlations are listed. See Appendix D for the full specification and source of the characteristics.
Source: The dependent variable is calculated from the 2001 Census SMS, Table MG109. Crown copyright

Finally, the Bristol case is distinctive in having only one of the 40 or so characteristics that is correlated at a statistically significant level (down to 5%) with its 34 localities' in/out ratios for the 'Higher managerial and professional' group. This is for the level of owner-occupation. The next highest correlations were positive ones with household income, presence of people in intermediate occupations and employment rate among working-age people, and negative ones with people living in housing association accommodation and people born outside the European Union.

These correlation analyses provide a pretty clear idea of the types of places that are most favoured by members of the 'Higher managerial and professional' class that moved between localities in the pre-census year. The picture is similar for all three city regions and rather predictable, even if the specific characteristics highlighted by the correlations vary somewhat between the three in strength. Far more of this group were entering than leaving localities that had the highest proportions of well-off people as indicated by the high correlations with such related characteristics as social grade AB, household income and owner-occupation. This group also tends to shun localities with high representation of manual occupations, crime, people lacking qualifications, people with limiting long-term illness, rented accommodation and immigrants from outside the EU.

These correlations by themselves, however, are not able to tell us anything more specific about the drivers of these patterns of migration. In very largely telling a single story, it is not obvious which of these characteristics are of most importance when all the likely factors are taken into account at the same time. Moreover, once the effect of this broad set of social factors is isolated, it may be found that some other factors that are not highly correlated with the overall migration patterns play some part. To test this, we applied multiple regression analysis to the in/out ratios. For this purpose, we use a reduced list of variables, selecting from the 40 or so used in the correlation analysis just 15 that cover the full set of determinants identified above and generally represent groups of variables that are highly correlated with each other. This approach was taken so that the various models can be compared on a more equal footing, rather than models seeming to be different just because they contain variables with different names (but which are highly correlated and so represent the same underlying factors). The results are presented in Chapter 5.

G

Appendix: Issues for further research

This appendix tackles two related questions. Given the several new features of the Census in 2001 and the various data issues described in the study, how much confidence can be placed in the findings presented in this report? Second, where gaps remain in our knowledge, what would seem the best way forward for remedying these and, more specifically, how much more insight could we expect to derive from further analysis of census data as opposed to drawing on other sources?

The first question is particularly appropriate in a situation where the work is in many ways experimental and exploratory. Such is the plethora of innovations in the 2001 Census – the One Number Census, the small cell adjustment method of disclosure control, term-time address rather than parental home for students, the moving group concept, no usual address one year ago and a completely new socioeconomic classification, to name just a few (see Appendix A) – that it has felt like studying a completely new source.

As we do not have access to the sorts of data needed to measure the effects of these methodological and definitional changes, the most obvious route open to us for validating our results is checking how far they conform to expectations derived from previous studies and associated theory and, where differences are detected, looking for supporting evidence from other sources. The bottom line is that our main findings are pretty much in line with the results of the most comparable work carried out on previous censuses (Champion and Fisher, 2003). This is in spite of covering three times as many cities, including smaller ones that might have been expected to have performed more strongly in migration terms than the general picture for the large conurbations studied previously – admittedly, a few did, but more were little different. The biggest departure from the previous results is London's very strong performance in terms of its migration exchanges of occupationally classified people, especially the 'Higher managerial and professional' cadre. Yet this was presaged in the 1981 and 1991 Census data that showed London attracting and retaining professionals to a greater extent than other large cities and, moreover, as noted in Chapter 2, the capital has undergone a major transformation in fortunes over the past couple of decades.

This general confirmation of the validity of our results lends support, in particular, to the use of the moving group concept as the basis for tabulating the socioeconomic complexion of migration. As the equivalent tables in the 1981 and 1991 Censuses had been for counts of all persons, we were initially worried that our results would have been distorted by being only for the reference persons of moving groups (MGRPs). That this does not seem to be the case probably reflects the fact that fully two thirds of moving groups nationally comprise just one person and that a sizeable proportion of the other members of multi-person moving groups are aged under 16 and are not relevant to our analysis of migration by occupation-based types. Also, the number of migrants living in communal establishments – who, by definition, do not belong to moving groups – is also known to be relatively small. On the other hand, there is one serious downside to the moving group concept, in that there is no obvious denominator available for calculating migration rates, prompting us to resort to the use of in/out ratios. There is scope for further research to test whether the total number of residents living in households, despite not being capable of representation as moving groups, would be an adequate proxy of the 'population at risk'.

One area that we are less confident about, however, is gauging the impact of migration on cities' human capital and hence it is one that we have, reluctantly, decided not to attempt. We would have liked to have calculated the net effect of within-UK migration on the stock of each of our four occupational types, but we knew from the outset that it would not be possible to do this in an accurate and meaningful way. Obviously from what has just been said, the moving group has been one impediment due to its less than complete tabulation of individual migrants by National Statistics Socioeconomic Classification (NS-SEC). Far more serious, however, is the fact that this type of calculation can be made only if it is assumed that people have not changed in their relevant characteristics during the pre-census year or, alternatively, would have changed in the same way whether or not they had changed address. This is not a new problem in that the census has never asked anything about people's circumstances one year earlier except for their address then, and it failed to do so in 2001 despite a strong case being made by users for a question about people's economic position one year ago, including whether a person had been a student then (Rees, 1998).

Even though we have steered clear of measuring the net effect of migration on cities, the absence of information about people's labour market position and occupation one year ago has still posed difficulties in the interpretation of our results. The biggest single issue concerns students who graduated in the year before the census and will thus be classified by their NS-SEC status, which – unless they have continued in full-time study – will, in terms of the categories used in our study, mean one of the four occupation-based groupings or 'other unclassified'. We have had to be aware that a proportion of those recorded as leaving our 27 cities in the pre-census year and classified by NS-SEC at the census will have been full-time students before their move, but from the available data we cannot identify these separately from people who were making the same move but changing jobs. In discussing this issue in relation to longer-distance migration to London from the other 26 cities (see Chapter 4), we have made the point that, whether or not they had jobs as full-time students, their departure on graduation represents a loss of potential human capital for the university cities. Even so, given the importance accorded to the challenge of graduate retention nowadays (see, for instance, GLA Economics, 2004; Scottish Executive, 2004), it would be very helpful to be able to focus in on this component of cities' migration balance and, further, to develop a set of migration accounts that enables the departure of recent graduates to be set against the arrival of freshers that can be identified from the 2001 Census data. Assuming that most graduating students are aged around 22 at the time of the census, one step forward would be through commissioning the census agencies to generate a version of Table MG109 that provided a breakdown by age.

Other types of transitions in the migration year leading up to the census are likely to be far less significant. As regards departures from the labour force through retirement, the situation is very different from entering it from full-time study, as the majority of people who left the labour force within the previous 12 months are likely to have followed the census form's advice to enter details of their most recent job, in which case they will have been classified by occupation (unless aged 75 or over at the census; see Appendix A). Admittedly, these people no longer considered themselves as part of the labour force at the time of the census, so we cannot analyse one year of change in a labour market accounting framework. For the purposes of studying the social composition of migration, however, it is appropriate to have them categorised on the basis of this last job. Even in terms of studying changes in the labour force skills available to cities, there is a case for including them in the data on cities' migration exchanges, given that many departures from the labour force are merely temporary (as is well documented for women with young children) and retirement is a much more fluid process than it used to be.

The other main type of transition is people changing jobs in the pre-census year. It is likely that migrants who change job at the same time as they move home are more likely to change their occupational status than non-migrants changing jobs, and that this would especially be the case for those considering it worthwhile to make a longer-distances move. Nevertheless, it is probably safe to assume that the majority of the migrants that we have analysed did not change the skill level of their job or, perhaps more arguably, that they might have changed in the same way without migrating, even if that change may not have occurred quite as quickly. This is another area that merits further investigation using a data source that already asks about people's jobs one year ago as well as about their address then. For the future, it would be very helpful if the next census in 2011 could do this. In the meantime, we have attempted to minimise the effect of such transitions by using just four broad occupational groups.

One way of trying to get a better idea of the nature of these transitions and the effect they have on cities is through the Office for National Statistics (ONS) Longitudinal Study, using the records for individual people that have been matched between censuses. As mentioned previously, Fielding (1992) has used this to great effect in examining migration between the 'escalator region' of South East England and the rest of England and Wales. Williams and Champion (1998) have also used it to assess the impact of in-migration on the labour market performance of a depressed regional economy, focusing on the case of Cornwall and the rest of the South West. Obviously, over a 10-year period between censuses, it is difficult to be exact about how closely linked in timing and causation is any change in address with that in occupation, but at least by having details of labour market position, occupation and so on for both before and after the migration (as well as for non-migrants), it is possible to assess the impact of such longer-term population movements on local economies. In the context of individual cities as opposed to larger regions, the 1% sample size is a limiting factor, but partly offsetting this is the fact that a 10-year period generates far more migrants than the one year before the census and that a full decade will be generalising across a range of conditions in contrast to the pre-census year relating to what is essentially a snapshot at one point in an economic cycle.